Strategic Organizational Alignment

Strategic Organizational Alignment

Authority, Power, Results

Chris Crosby

Edited by John Hanlen

BUSINESS EXPERT PRESS

First published in 2017 by
Business Expert Press, LLC
222 East 46th Street, New York, NY 10017
www.businessexpertpress.com

ISBN-13: 978-1-63157-660-7 (print)
ISBN-13: 978-1-63157-661-4 (e-book)

Business Expert Press Strategic Management Collection

Collection ISSN: 2150-9611 (print)
Collection ISSN: 2150-9646 (electronic)

Cover and interior design by S4Carlisle Publishing Services Private Ltd., Chennai, India
Graphics created by Chris Crosby

First edition: 2017

10 9 8 7 6 5 4 3 2 1

Printed in the United States of America

To John, Robert, Gilmore, and Merlyn.
Thank you for your love and support!

Abstract

Business results, major change, project initiatives—can be achieved more easily than imagined.

Strategic Organizational Alignment shows you how and points out the reasons why most excuses businesses make for inadequate implementations are wrong.

Through stories, illustrations, and step-by-step guides Crosby shows you a simple, profound, and repeatable way to ensure your business aligns its employees and has a clear path to success.

Keywords

alignment, business results, change, change management, cross-functional, leadership, MBA, organization development, organizational development, productivity, project management, stanford, workplace

Advanced Quotes for *Strategic Organizational Alignment: Authority, Power, Results*

"Using the principles outlined here, Mr. Crosby helped us to successfully implement Oracle in six locations, spanning four countries, Korea, The Philippines, China, and Hong Kong, by all measures, a very successful implementation."

—Sunny Liu
Finance Director, APAC, CSI.

"Mr. Crosby helped us utilize the theory outlined in *Strategic Organizational Alignment* allowing us to launch six major new products compared with zero in the prior year. We have since repeated the success and now have a consistent stream of new products being launched, thanks to this new approach."

—Clive Copsey,
V.P. New Product Development and R&D—Sabert Corp

". . . A very good hands-on reference for those involved in change"
". . . a good solid nuts-and-bolts explanation of the key roles in successful change efforts from a professional with hands on experience . . . It is simple, relevant, and most importantly, it just works. I like it a lot."

—Matt Minahan
2015 Chair, Board of Trustees
Organization Development Network

"The book outlines critical principles I use to lead my organizations. It is effective, practical, and balanced. An important contribution to any leader, manager, or change agent"

—Brian Bauerbach
President & CEO, Mold Rite Plastics

"Powerful, practical, and most importantly, what I did to help each business that I was in charge of to succeed!"

—John Nicol
Partner and General Manager, Microsoft

"Chris created the change structures and processes we used for our global Oracle v11i implementation (26 modules) to engage the business and effectively work through all project issues. He then led the effort that helped us transition from region to region, plant to plant, and culture to culture with ease. The result: zero-missed shipments in a project that implemented at 18 locations spanning 7 countries. Plus, satisfied end users! Chris is an excellent collaborator, educator, facilitator, business leader, and communicator. He made a huge difference for our team, the go-live locations, and our business."

—Mark Howard
Project Manager, EBS (Oracle)

"*Strategic Organizational Alignment* is an important book that every leader should read. Rather than giving simple solutions or a fancy new model, Crosby recognizes that sustained performance is only achieved by diligent attention to the basics. In this engaging and clearly written book, he shows how challenging that is and then provides detailed actions that can truly align the organization. This is not for the faint-hearted, but for the leader who truly seeks excellence."

—David L. Bradford,
The Eugene D. O'Kelly II Senior Lecturer in Leadership, Emeritus at the Stanford University Graduate School of Business and co-author (with Allan R. Cohen) of the best-selling book, Power Up: Transforming Organizations through Shared Leadership

Contents

The Assessments in Appendix A, additional SATA examples, and my Organization Development (OD) roots are available online at Business Expert Press.

List of Figures

Preface

"Project overruns are eating up our budget!"
"We know the problem, and it ain't our department!"
"Nothing happens here unless the manager of X says so!"
"I know the project was a disaster; I am just happy it got done!"
"I don't know what he said, but whatever it is, I don't believe it!"
"It's the hierarchy: it takes too many layers to get anything done!"
"We are too flat: everybody does whatever they want!"

The voice of dissatisfaction echoes in many organizations. The statements above have a common denominator: they come from employees in misaligned workplaces that are failing to meet mission-critical objectives.

Most employees in organizations can point to a new structure, procedure, software development, R&D project, merger, or acquisition that did not live up to expectations or, worse, completely failed. Who has not heard of such disasters? Even potentially transformational practices such as lean manufacturing, Six Sigma, and new problem-solving techniques fail at alarming rates. Understanding how to use your authority and power to truly align your organization is the solution to such failures. *Strategic Organizational Alignment* is built on this and uses as its foundation major components of Organization Theory. I contend that failure in most cases is not the change, project, decision to merge, or choice of initiative: Rather, it is one of execution.

The unfortunate news, however, is that most companies also do not recognize *where* they are falling short. Instead of looking at how their organization is functioning as a whole, they decide the issue is with something else: new techniques, new structures, the people, the union, the management—you name it—the norm is blame and an outward focus.

This book is for those in organizations who are willing to take the more difficult yet rewarding path of *ownership* and *admittance* that they are at least part of the problem. Ownership *is* the path to learning.

In the coming pages you will learn how to utilize the existing strengths *already within* your organization. To align and execute, you will learn how to understand and leverage authority, generative power, and organization theory. Once you do that, you will increase your bottom-line results.

Organization Theory is based on systems thinking and lets no person off the hook. In fact, in every organization all have a role to play and must learn how to play it well or failure will ensue. Many think that projects, issues, and actions get successfully resolved or implemented by heroic acts. Therefore, success or failure is dependent on whether they have the right people, rather than looking at the relationships between the people. In contrast, Organization Theory is a series of constructs that explain how all organizations function. The major categories I focus on include: (1) the reality of authority, (2) an analysis tool called Sponsor/Agent/Target/Advocate, (3) decision clarity, and (4) accountability.

Who is the book for?

This book is written for those in organizations working to achieve results. It is for **the CEO, the Manager, the Project Manager, the Organization Development Consultant**, and anyone else who must maneuver within the boundaries of a workplace. It is a must for functions that constantly cross groups such as Quality, Safety, Maintenance, Human Resources, Engineering, or external consultants of any type. It is for all layers, so it is also for production employees or workers, ready to more appropriately use their influence to help their business succeed.

This book is not a new program, a new model, or a group of suggested organizational structures. The book is intended to help you succeed at whatever task, project, or deliverable you are trying to accomplish within your workplace by pointing out the authority and power dynamics that exist. Once these are understood, then your organization has a better chance of getting aligned towards improving results.

The story of Jane, Joe, and Ed

I have written a story to introduce each chapter and help you understand further the *what, why,* and *how* to use this book. Although the book is filled with step-by-step instructions, the story helps ground them in real-world situations. The story itself is about a large insurance company that develops its own software for its carriers. What happens in the story comes directly from my experience. Although the names are fictitious, the situations are real.

While the narrative context involves a "large project," these concepts apply to every situation, large or small, in all organizations. This book is about how to align your organization to its goals including improvements to day-to-day work processes. What you are about to learn, I use to align workplaces that manufacture products, do non-profit work, and in high tech settings. I have used it in organizations all over the world including Asia, South America, and Europe.

The goal of this book is to help organizations become more aligned, one conversation at a time. The story shows some of those conversations. What I aim for here are direct, straightforward, and honest conversations about realities that are inside all organizations. Which I then hope is followed by insight, and the right people at the right places in the organization beginning to function in ways that will shift the organization towards greater success.

The chapters

Chapter 1 outlines a theory of authority in the workplace and becomes the frame for the rest of the book. Chapter 2 is about setting clear goals. Chapter 4 goes hand-in-hand with the earlier chapters, delineating types of power and, most importantly, *generative power:* the heart of this book.

In other words, once you learn about and understand how to use your generative power, it becomes the catalyst to lead your employees, increase their engagement, and focus them on the right goals to achieve results. Chapters 3, 5, and 6 go in depth on how to analyze your existing situation and develop strategies to get all impacted managers and employees moving in the same direction. From that point on, the book explores how to use workplace knowledge effectively, how to *truly* empower your employees, and, perhaps most importantly, how to effectively follow-up.

If at any point you think I want you to start a new program or I am pushing a new model, stop. I am not advocating either of those things. Many are looking for the perfect model or theory to improve their workplace. The truth is that although some are better than others, "perfect" does not exist. This book helps you look at whatever you are doing and highlights factors that need to be addressed in order to succeed. These factors are universal, cross-cultural, and exist in every workplace.

The coming chapters derive from my extensive training in Organization Development and my long experience working in businesses. I have worked the most with intact work groups (boss and employees) from the lowest levels all the way up to the CEO. You could call what you are about to read the nuts and bolts of change; moreover, it is the key to successful day-to-day work.

My training helped me to become aware of the realities of authority and dynamics of power in all organizations and how to help clients utilize them to create thriving work environments. When I have applied what I learned to projects, whole-system change, process improvements, work-team developments, conflict resolutions, and software implementations, the results have been consistent: business success. As you read on, you will learn some overarching aspects of all workplaces: the key to organization health and results achievement.

Introduction

Your business success depends on how well you and your employees interact so that *everyone* in each department gets *what* they need, *when* they need it. This fact is not a problem, rather it is a reality to embrace and *strive* towards perfecting.

Strategic Organizational Alignment is built on this.

If instead of embracing this reality, you fight against it, then you likely are struggling to complete major projects, initiatives, or goals on-time, with quality, or within budget.

Once you think other people, departments, or functions are the problem, then you miss the point. Align, support, take pride in how you work together, and unify your interactions with the customer. Then you will reach business results never before imagined!

My mission is to help organizations align and focus on what is truly important to reach their objectives, then to provide them with the implementation tools for achievement. This is not some slogan or a new program; neither of those things work. Rather it is about highlighting dynamics that currently exist within your workplace, and giving you the tools to leverage them. In most cases, **the main tool that you need to succeed is the people already inside your organization**. This book shows you how to *align them* to your strategic direction and to *involve them* to get there.

In the coming chapters I will show you how to organize and align your workplace to consistently achieve a high level of business success. If there is a secret, it is that there is no one right tool external to your workplace. The answer lies within. The challenge is to tap into the collective wisdom of your employees in order to create a thriving, productive workplace!

The Four Key Ingredients for Success:

1. **Set clear goals:** Clear goals are measurable, balanced, realistic, and achievable. Chapter 2 of this book is about workplace goals. Ironically, many managers do not even have goals for their work group, let alone know the goals for the rest of the business. Also, many do not know the difference between an *action*, a *standard*, and a *goal* (p. 22). There are many tools in the market such as the balanced scorecard, lean manufacturing's A4, or Robert Crosby's "Rainbow Model of Goals" to help develop and clarify workplace goals, but none are very useful unless they are accompanied by a process to engage and align your workplace. Employees should know the current state of their business in the marketplace, their work groups' goals, their individual goals, and how they integrate into the bigger picture of the organization. Armed with that knowledge, workers have a much easier time becoming productive contributors.

2. **Align your workplace:** The focus of this book is how to align your workplace. It is a never-ending job but can and should have precision around critical tasks, projects, and initiatives. Chapters 3, 5, and 6 lay out step-by-step instructions, and the theoretical underpinnings of how to align your workplace. Since there is a lack of knowledge of how to truly align workplaces, most spend months or years to improve items that could be accomplished in days or weeks. Many send out Change Agents to do the work that should be done by aligned bosses (Sponsors) once they are educated as to how to drive their goals. It is not rocket science but it does take hard work, commitment and, most of all, *it takes an engaged leader to create an engaged workplace.* If a leader sits back and waits, guess what? Nothing or at least not much will happen.

3. **Engage the right employees when solving problems:** Engagement is more than just a buzz word. It is the key to making sure the right knowledge is being utilized to solve your business issues. *Do not engage because of an ideology or just because somebody told you so!* Analyze each work scenario and ensure that you involve a balance of workers, managers, and technical experts in the areas that you are trying to improve. They all have critical inputs for solving work problems.

The mistake many make is forgetting to involve the people doing the work when solving problems. This book is about creating clear strategies for involving the right people, at the right time, to create better solutions to the challenges facing your workplace.

4. **Follow through until you are consistently achieving results:** This is the area where many, if not most, fail. The ability to stay focused until you are getting results is hard work and requires constant focus to make sure your workplace is aligned and working towards goals. There are simple ways to follow-up on tasks and initiatives which I outline in Chapter 10 of this book (p. 147), but most leaders lose focus. Personal authority (p. 75), the capability to use your personal authority (p. 218), diligence, and solid structures (Chapter 8, p. 123) are the keys to doing this well.

If you can learn how to consistently achieve in these four key areas, you will reach high-level business results. This book is intended to help you do just that.

Our Story Begins

Joe, the company CEO, sat back in his chair and breathed a huge sigh of relief. *Wow! I can't believe we finally found her. After an executive search of many months, the product manager we need to push through our most critical initiative is finally here. Now I can begin to breathe easy and let it happen. Ed, the VP of Technology, is already getting her acclimated and settled in. We really hit the nail here: perfect fit, great technical skills combined with a go-getter attitude. What was it her reference said: "No obstacle is too big for her to push through." Why can't we find more people like this? Isn't there a global recession? Oh, well, now she is here, let the project proceed . . .*

◊◊◊

Ed sat down and exhaled. As VP of Research and Design, he has been feeling a great deal of pressure to deliver on a project that would make a difference. Now they have such a project and the right person to pull it off. *OK, I think this is gonna work! Finally we found her and she seems to have all the right stuff. Bright, technically gifted, and filled with drive. I think this one just might save my job and department. We haven't hit on a major project for a while and marketing assures me that this is the 'one' that will help us capture back market share. My major work is done: I have briefed Jane on the project, told her about the key players, and walked her around the business. I can't wait for her to start whipping this business into shape . . .*

◊◊◊

Jane sat back and smiled. *Wow, unbelievable! I did it, I landed my dream job! Executive Product Manager at an established high-tech firm. No more crazy start-up adventures in businesses that haven't a clue. These guys have been doing this for years and are at the top of the industry. All we have to do is succeed on the project for which I was initially hired. Ha! We will put the rest of the competition in the dust! Bye bye!*

So where is that list? Oh yeah, here it is. Hmm, I need to talk to John Snyder, Francis, and Javier to begin to work on the project. Great! Lets get going!

"Hey, John, got a minute?" Jane said.

"Minute? For what?" replied John.

"I am Jane Powell, hired to work on the SMART project."

"The what project?" John said, looking confused. "The SMART project. I haven't heard about that, so why do you need to talk to me?"

Jane immediately felt a little discomfort. "Well, you are a key player and your department plays a huge role in its implementation."

"What? My department." Now John was starting to feel pressure. "Look Jane, no offense, but we are booked solid for the next several months. I couldn't possible help you . . ."

Jane left then, feeling a little frustrated but still determined. She then walked into Francis's office. "Hi Francis, I am Jane, the new product manager on the SMART project."

"The what? We hired a new manager? And for what project? I have not heard of that."

And so it went. . . .

In conversation after conversation, almost nobody knew. Most seemed not to care, as if they worked in a different business.

Jane thought, *Wow, I must quickly speak with Ed; this is serious.*

◊◊◊

Later that same day in Ed's office . . . "Really? Most knew nothing? How can that be? I sent out the standard email?"

"Hmm. This place is a mess; it has always been this way. Good thing we have a great product or we would be toast. But now we are in trouble. Jane, you are going to have to help straighten us out. I have an idea. I have been recommended a consultant who, according to my good friend, focuses on different things most of us may be blind to. From what I have heard, he gets results, as in real business results. My friend said he helped them hit on six new projects in 1 year when they hadn't successfully accomplished a project in several years."

"Wow, six up from zero?" quipped Jane.

"Yup, that is what he said. Yet, I have been too reluctant to call him, you know, seems like a weakness to ask for help. But, Jane, we need it: we have got to hit on this project or we will start failing and that means layoffs and pain."

Jane spoke "OK, let's call him . . ."

"Hi, Jane. Hi, Ed. Very nice to meet you. My name is Tim. How can I help?"

"Well, Tim, here is the story . . ." Jane then proceeded to tell about her hire, her excitement, and the immediate road blocks.

Tim listened carefully, asked a few questions for clarity, then said, "Sounds like your system is way out of alignment: people are working on different things and authority is running rampant. I have some good news and bad news. First, the good. You can and will fix this. I have seen it all before and there are clear things to do to solve these problems. Now the bad news: this is going to be really hard and will take persistence and patience. There is no magic bullet to any organization's ills, but there are clear, concrete, specific things to do in all cases. Knowing this, do you want to proceed?"

Jane and Ed talked, then turned back to Tim. "We don't have any choice: our employees are counting on us to do this. Please help!"

"OK, it would be an honor. Let's start by talking about a dimension that I think is critical to align your organization. Also Ed, for a change this big to work, it will be very important that your CEO be part of the transformation. Can you bring him to the next session?"

Ed looked pensive and uncertain. He sat up straight when he talked. "Tim, I can ask him to come, but why do you think he should join us? I mean, Joe is really busy; between the board and his lead team there is not much more that he can put on his plate."

"Well, Ed, that's a great question. You told me this project is huge and mission critical, correct? I mean that if it fails you are in trouble in a number of ways."

"Yes!" Jane and Ed said simultaneously.

"Then if that is the case he does need to be highly informed and leading the organization. I mean, I know CEOs are theoretically responsible for everything in their business. Yet, of course, they must rely on the people below them, at each level, to do their part. However, for something this big to really succeed, most CEOs would need to drive clear objectives and goals throughout their organizations. Joe has a unique position that is critical to alignment: all departments report up through him. I could just work with you and Jane, but that would make it much harder to succeed."

Ed spoke, his eyes twinkling with knowing, "Aha, yes! That is it: all we need is for Joe to tell everyone to get in line, and then all is well. Why didn't I think of that?"

Eyes narrowing, Tim said, "Well, not exactly, Ed. Let me further explain what I mean." He went on to say, "If you get strong leadership from top to bottom in your organization, then you dramatically increase your chance at excellence. Calm *generative power* (see p. 71) creates healthy well-functioning organizations where employees can be straight about all work scenarios and conversations are more direct and constructive."

Ed spoke up again, "Yes! Like I said, Joe will just tell the employees how to do it and all will be OK!"

"No, Ed! That is not what I meant when I said 'top to bottom.' Joe needs to align the organization around the goals, yet he also needs to give people significant freedom, within boundaries of course, to achieve those goals. I will explain more in a minute but this is a critical point. What you thought of when I said 'top to bottom' sounds like an organization that is too autocratic. This is about managing from the middle, setting boundaries, significantly engaging and allowing for the employees to really thrive."

"Wow, Tim," Ed said. "This is starting to sound exciting."

"Yes!" Jane also responds.

"Very good," Tim continued. "Managers need to be aligned around goals, work processes and even who is doing what tasks, while employees need the *appropriate* freedom to go about their work. The employees also need to be involved in continuously improving the work processes or you will get processes put in place that are stuck and hurting the organization."

"Ed, I am afraid that if your CEO is not on board with a project this big, you'll spend undue time on many small issues of misalignment and find your project being late, over-budget and lacking in the standard of quality you need to get a leg up on the competition."

"Tim, say no more. I get it and will talk to Joe. He did say he would be happy to help in any way he can. It's just that I know he has a lot on his plate. By the way, Tim: for Joe to join us next week, is there anything I should prep him with?"

"Yes, Ed," Tim said. "I am just about to address authority in systems. Why don't you give Joe a copy of my new book and have him read Chapter One? Both you and Jane may also have a copy if you would like. In that way, you'll know what I asked Joe to read. If he does not get to it, all won't be lost."

Tim handed them the books while saying, "If you would like to, you can read Chapter One later to get a nice recap about authority in systems." From there he walked to his whiteboard and wrote the phrase "Too Autocratic"; then, quite a distance from it, he wrote the phrase "Too Permissive"; after that, he drew a line between them.

Let me talk about the realities of authority. What I am about to say exists in every organization on the planet. The reality is that it is there. The other reality is that most are either afraid to or don't want to acknowledge that it exists. *They think, for instance, that it is 'old school' to be autocratic and 'new school' to be permissive with your employees. For me, both of those beliefs are 'as old as the hills.'* What is probably more accurate is that in order to be somewhere in-between, you have to first acknowledge that authority exists and then learn about its realities. From there you can make a conscious choice to manage between the two extremes. Balancing between the extremes of authority is a never-ending task and can be difficult. Yet it brings with it the potential of creating a workplace where employees are truly engaged, and have the appropriate authority to act on their own in each situation they need to in order to reach the businesses results. *I am not talking about heroic acts in a dysfunctional system; I am talking about a functional system that has clearly defined goals and boundaries.* But make no mistake, it takes work and commitment to get there."

Ed adds, "And the rewards?"

"Simple," Tim responds. "When it really happens you get high morale and record results."

Tim, Jane, and Ed then continued the conversation . . .

◊◊◊

Read Chapter One

CHAPTER 1

Authority

"There is no more important area to be clear about in organizations than the reality and presence of authority. Miss this one and you will forever have to make up reasons for why things fail. When you get it right, change, people, processes, and–above all–business results will fall into place."

Authority for many is a dirty word. The truth is it is just a word and it is present in every organization. Some think the word "boss" or "manager" is a problem; the reason is psychological. To be alive is to be raised, and we were all raised by people. In other words, we were all born into an authority system. All of us had a primary caregiver or two who did their best to raise us in the way they thought would help us function well in society.

This process, called socialization, includes how we exist in the world from basics like walking across the street at crosswalks, manners, and even how we think about doing chores such as mowing the lawn or cleaning. Socialization also teaches us basic social etiquette tasks such as speaking with respect to people despite not wanting to, and countless other behaviors, all taught so that we can behave appropriately in society.

Socialization is both overtly taught and indirectly learned. Many lessons are given through direct instruction like "Say please," after someone gives you a gift or "Look both ways," prior to crossing the street. There are also indirect lessons learned through your life experiences. The voice tone used when you are told to clean your room, or the things you witnessed when family members were in conflict, all left an imprint on you.

This imprint is especially strong when it comes to your relationship and beliefs about authority. We all depended on an authority taking care of us in each moment of our first preverbal years. In fact, depending on how we were parented, we may think favorably or negatively about authority. We will surely have some beliefs about parenting or being a boss. This range is impossible to fully identify, but I have met people who think bosses should be kind and gentle and people who think bosses should be tough and unapologetic. Whatever the belief, it came from our unique history and, if left unexplored, will likely color your view of your current boss.

Despite this, the function of boss in any organization is critical for the work to get coordinated and completed. In fact, the word *boss* is just a word, but many put all sorts of judgments onto it. It is no wonder, out of such a potentially charged arena, that extreme ideas like trying to eliminate all bosses arise.

Robert P Crosby is an Organization Development (OD) practitioner who developed a theory about how authority works in systems. He was trained by the early pioneers in Organization Development in theories about the realities of authority within all organizations. He spent his career helping organizations thrive by getting clarity on authority and, thus paradoxically, helping employees gain more freedom to act in their jobs. He also helped many businesses like Alcoa at Addy, Washington recover from hardline fundamental stands against authority where people thought that taking away all bosses and trying to create a consensus culture would answer all their problems.

The unfortunate reality of such experiments is that ultimately the system cannot move, and chaos rather than clarity reigns.

Crosby Theory of Authority in Systems

Robert Crosby was heavily influenced by two seminal thinkers in the twentieth century: Kurt Lewin (1890 to 1947) and John Dewey (1859 to 1952). Not only did he study their works, but he was also trained by colleagues of John Dewey and one of Kurt Lewin's top graduate students, Ronald Lippitt. For 29 years, starting in 1957, Lippitt was his mentor and colleague. *Both Dewey and Lewin believed that democracy is a learned behavior.* Further, it is more difficult to learn than either autocracy or permissive styles of leadership.

When they used the word democracy they meant the ability to manage from the middle of the two extremes of too autocratic and too permissive. Further, ironically, they claimed that all employees know how to behave in either of the extremes. In contrast, when a leader starts managing from the middle, then a different type of learning must take place. That learning involves more effective communication and engagement of your employees and finding an appropriate balance of decision making and accountability.

Suddenly it is not all about the leader; one cannot hide behind the crowd. True employee empowerment comes from clarity of authority and appropriate delegation to the employees so that they have the ability to act fast and think for themselves. The balance here is that with such authority, employees must also increase their responsibility and be held accountable, or you risk a misaligned organization.

This puts a different premium on leaders: Now they must let go some of their decision authority and coach or mentor people to use good judgment. Of course, the permissive leaders have to do the opposite. They must take back the reins in certain areas and drive task and decision clarity. Both styles must begin leading in a way that engages people and drives clarity and accountability throughout the system. Thus, the art of leadership is to be able to tread the middle between these extremes in order to drive direction and empowerment throughout the organization. This, however, takes commitment to learning which includes education, skill practice, and persistence.

The payback is twofold. Most employees long for a real challenge and already know what to do in any given situation. They are just waiting to actually be given the chance. Engage them differently and morale will shoot up after the initial shock of the change. People processes will also improve as employees are given legitimate authority to do their tasks. This transition is not easy and won't happen without a true commitment.

To understand this further lets return to some classic studies on how different leadership styles impact their followers. Through Ronald Lippitt, Crosby learned of a surprising problem in Dr. Lippitt and R.K. White's 1930's classic studies of authority in boys' groups, conducted under Kurt Lewin's guidance. Lippitt told him that he sometimes had to lead the democratic group himself because the people who were asked to do so behaved permissively. That is why one sees the young Ron Lippitt himself on the classic black and white film. In fact, the original study was to see the difference between how the boys behaved under autocratic and democratic leaders. *The dilemma with the word "democracy" is that when asked to do it, most people act it out in a permissive way.*

Thus, their first "new discovery" was that the leaders who attempted to be democratic usually slipped into permissive forms of leadership. Thus, they added laissez-faire to the study. This highlighted Lewin's claim that democracy is a learned behavior and must be taught anew in each generation. As stated above, the contrast that was first studied by Lippitt (White joined him the second year) was between autocracy and democracy. That original experiment, upon analysis, yielded the powerful and classic continuum of authority: autocracy on one end and laissez-faire (permissive) on the other (p. 186).

Beyond the classic continuum on authority, there were other important discoveries. In 1939, *Patterns of aggressive behavior in experimentally created "social climates,"* was published by Kurt Lewin, Ronald Lippitt, and Ralph K. White in the Journal of Social Psychology. The studies were created to understand the effect of different leadership styles on the social climate of the groups. In other words, how did each leadership style impact both the behavior of the kids to each other and outputs produced by the groups.

The outcomes were as follows. The autocratic group produced the most, slightly more than the democratic group, and the least was produced in the laissez-faire (permissive) group. However, the quality of the product was the best in the democratically led group. In terms of social climate (morale), the most aggressive behavior recorded, regarding how they treated each other, was in the autocratic group. Surprisingly, the permissive group was a close second. In other words, the democratically led group produced the highest morale and the best quality product. Yet, as noted on the previous page, it was the hardest to find a person to lead becuase they had a tendency to slide into laisez-faire style leadership.

Apply this to organizations, and it becomes clear that democracy belongs mostly near the middle of the two extremes. It amounts to managing with the skills inherent in consultative and delegative styles of decision making while retaining the capacity to make independent decisions when needed. The latter is frequently needed in any management role. These ground-breaking studies indicate the tendency to confuse democracy with permissiveness. Lewin found that the advantages of managing from the middle are little known or understood.

Instead, there has been a largely unconscious movement among OD consultants, HR managers, and leaders in industry who believe that permissive ways of managing are superior, that they supposedly create better business results, and are of a higher order of maturity. Laissez-faire allows for total freedom of almost any action. Ironically, this creates either a workplace with little structure and unclear boundaries or a decision structure so rigid that no decisions get made because anyone has the power to veto them.

Autocracy normally involves a rigid order imposed by the top leader. It tends to create an organization with low employee empowerment and, ironically, pockets of permissiveness. Of course, the larger the organization gets, the harder it is for order to be imposed from the top, and attempts to do so often create the unintended consequence of stifling leaders of operational locations.

Democracy attempts to balance the two by creating the right amount of structure and distributing leadership among all formal leaders in the organization as well as by allowing for appropriate decision authority for each employee. To this end, White and Lippitt state: "To keep this (democracy as merely being a balance between two extremes) from being quite such an oversimplification, it should be added immediately that there is a third dimension consisting of friendly, creative communication within the group, and that in this dimension democracy, as represented in the experiments, was high while both of the others were low." Thus, the consensus style of self-directed teams and/or reluctance of many leaders, HR, and OD people to clarify authority at work directly correlates with this classic study regardless of one's lack of knowledge about it. Beginning in the 1950s, under Lippitts' tutelage, Crosby quickly began to see that understanding the reality of authority and how it is manifested in each organization is a higher human developmental stage (see Chapter 14).

From here he started helping organizations to solve business problems while keeping an eye on and coaching leaders to more effectively use their authority to accomplish their goals. He has spent his life helping organizations learn how to manage from the middle. He has also helped workplaces recover from their ill-conceived experiments with autonomous work teams. What follows is Robert Crosby's unique theory of authority in systems.

In a nutshell: *Authority exists in all systems.* Even if you pretend it does not–by doing away with supervisors–it will still emerge. If a group has no formal boss, followers and leaders will still fall into place, but at random. (A good example of this, although extreme, is the novel *Lord of the Flies.*) Furthermore, don't kid yourself that a self-managed team has no boss. The layers above are still responsible for the team's performance. If a leaderless group is failing, they will either be corrected from above or they will drag the organization's performance down with them.

Rather than creating a vacuum of authority by eliminating supervisors or bosses, focus on creating clarity about authority of who can decide what, and encourage dialogue about work issues upward, downward, and across departments. This needs to be done in each intact work group (boss and direct reports) as well as across functions. In fact, think of clarifying authority as an ongoing task with no end, and with adjustments made as situations change. It should happen at all levels with the people closest to the work given the ability to make decisions quickly, so efficient work gets done. In other words, delegate as much authority as possible, with clarity about who decides and how they will be monitored.

Further, *don't be driven by an ideology.* The often repeated error here is to immediately (sometimes behind the guise of a new program) move every group from authoritarian leadership to permissive, as if all are the same. Use an evolutionary approach that takes into account the uniqueness of each group/crew and recognizes that some will work better with a more directive style, while some groups can be more successful working with little direction as long as goals and accountability are clear. All of Robert Crosby's business books highlight the folly of permissiveness as manifested in the notion of self-managed teams. The same is true of authoritarianism. A great example of his evolutionary approach can be seen in Chapter 4 of *Cultural Change in Organizations (CCIO)* entitled "Autonomy and Productivity."

Finally, *this is a journey without end.* As people become more capable, they need more decision authority in order for the organization to be as productive as possible, but always with clarity and accountability. Newer employees with little experience, of course, need more direction (as nicely modeled by Hersey and Blanchard's "Situational Leadership").

Let your employees have as much freedom as you can, but never do it suddenly without clarity in a way that creates chaos and power struggles. Authority is! It is not good, bad, right, or wrong. When an organization creates a vacuum by trying to eliminate supervisors, authority will arise in the workforce, sometimes for better but far too often for worse. It is too important to leave to chance!

Effective organizations are honest about authority and continually strive to find balance. A critical component of creating employee empowerment is for them to have the authority to act. The goal is for managers to give the employees maximum influence, including appropriate delegation, so that work can be accomplished with quality and on time. Yet managers must stay in touch with the results and quality of the work. Therefore, simple ways to monitor and continually assess whether the business objectives are being achieved are critical components of delegation and, ironically, are often overlooked.

Through increasing your knowledge of organization theory, you will gain a better understanding of how to utilize authority in your system. The next component of utilizing authority and stepping into strong leadership is creating clear goals. Chapter 2 is devoted to goals.

From there I will move to a theory critical to driving alignment within the legitimate authority in your system, called "Sponsor Agent Target Advocate." Daryl Conner is the creator of the model "Sponsor Agent Target Advocate," introduced in *Managing at the Speed of Change*. Yet, the version you will receive here is informed by Crosby's Theory of Authority in Systems. "Sponsor Agent Target Advocate," or SATA, the driving paradigm for all my work in organizations. In Chapter 12, I explore Crosby's "Decision-making Styles," the key to driving down authority throughout your system: intact work group (boss and direct reports) by intact work group.

What Are We Working Towards?

One week later, Ed and Jane went back to talk with Tim, and, as requested, Joe joined them. Joe looked pleased to be there, but the impatience growing within Ed was palatable. "OK, Tim, we listened to you last week and have each read the chapter, but I must say we are all a bit confused. What the heck does it really have to do with anything?"

"Jane has continued to have tough conversations; Joe here is starting to get very concerned; and I can't quite make sense out of anything."

Tim looked a little anxious as he spoke; after all, this was his first session with the CEO involved and he wanted it to go well, yet he also understood that he had to speak his truth. "Well, Ed, I need to first introduce you to how authority works within a business. From the initial stories, it sounds like you may be working in silos. People are not really talking things through, and they are not being held accountable to support all areas. Rather, they are caught up in their own areas, just trying to make things work. From my perspective, you may have a culture that is too permissive. If so, ironically, the leaders have to step up, and, Joe, you have a unique role in changing that dynamic, so I am glad you are here. Of course, you cannot do it alone; you must help all the leaders be more accountable to each other and their employees."

Joe, shifting in his seat and looking a little puzzled, said "Wait, too permissive? I hammer people all the time. Why just last week I—"

"Um, Joe," Tim cut in, "permissiveness and hammering people ironically often go hand-in-hand. The question is: Do you seek clarity and understanding with the right people, then truly empower them to drive results? I, of course, am not in your business but it sounds like clarity and alignment are not quite in place."

"Well," Joe spoke with some anxiety in his voice, "just yesterday I clarified with the shift leader on shift C that he must reach our quality targets. Oh, yeah, and I told him that he needs to make sure his people work safe! After all, his shift has had the worst safety record."

"Hmm Joe. I am talking about your direct reports, not the people who are way under you. For real alignment to happen, you must have critical conversations with your own reports in order for them to know the focus of the business. Reprimanding those that are in layers below you will only add confusion in your system. Manage your own people, and then help them manage their people as well: mostly with positive reinforcement but hold out to use appropriate reprimands when necessary. But, Joe, the reality is most people do not spend the time to have alignment conversations about issues critical for success. In order to change your workplace, you must begin to have those, and have them cascade, in an appropriate way, throughout your system."

"Hmm, but you don't understand. In my business, a few of my direct reports have been here since our inception, and they are strong. Not just strong, they know so much, I can't afford to lose them. How can I be tough with them?"

"Yes," Tim said, empathy in his voice, "that sounds difficult. However, for real change to happen, you must take the reins in appropriate ways. Truly difficult people do exist, but it is my experience that they are few and far between. Once you do the difficult work of alignment, then employees who seem difficult usually become much easier to manage. In fact, they may just be waiting for real direction."

Jane watched with much discomfort but finally jumped in. "But, Tim, it's not just his direct reports; there are many in this business who have to contribute to this project, yet hardly anyone even knows it exists."

Joe, feeling dejected, chimed in. "Wow, I guess I am just really messing this up."

Tim replied. "No, Joe, you are just doing what many do: being a bit too passive and hoping the workers figure it out. Most workers are smart enough to at least survive, but the challenge is how to get a workplace to thrive. That is not only possible, but probable when you follow certain steps. And yes, Joe, I get it that you have two very powerful lead-team members and are afraid of legacy data, but if you do not take the risk to really manage them, then you also risk never moving the organization forward. Forgive the cheesy analogy, but I am talking about backbone, Joe, yet it must be appropriate. Hammering people only in times of tension does not work. The only thing it does is add to the tension already there and begins to demoralize the workplace."

"Remember what you just read. Democracy—that is the ability to manage from the middle—needs to be learned anew in each generation. Most confuse democracy with permissiveness, then slip in between being too permissive and too autocratic. Joe, your examples fit this definition perfectly. The challenge is to learn how to be effective from the middle. Ironically, that means a much higher degree of interaction."

Joe through his slight frustration at Tim, suddenly had the following insight, "Wow, I sent Jane to go out and start managing the product, yet I had hardly talked to anyone about it. The board knows about it, Marketing knows because they suggested it, yet many in the business have no clue. Oh, Jane, I am so sorry. But it is not just you. I have been operating this way for years. I guess I am really not that clear on what to do."

"Well, you are probably clearer than you think, but, hey, this is why you are talking to me; I will do my best to guide you in solving your problems and surpassing your previous business records. This may be hard to believe but it is predictable. When my clients do an integrated strategy and really follow-up in the ways I can teach you, they reach new records."

Ed finally chimed in, "Records? Come on."

"Yes, Ed," said Tim. "Each time a full strategy is implemented, new records have been accomplished. The challenge is how to stay the course during follow through. I will show you simple ways to do so yet it will take diligence and determination to be successful."

Joe, seemingly at a different place, said, "OK, what's next? I can't afford to wait, and Lord knows I need the direction."

Tim smiled. "That is music to my ears!"

"Well," Tim continued, "the next thing I am curious about are your business goals. I know that Jane is your project manager (PM), but I am a little fuzzy from there."

Ed spoke up, "Jane is what? She is the Product Manager? She is not the project manager."

"Really?" Tim looked surprised. "Oh, well. Who is the project manager?"

Joe spoke up, "Project manager? Ed, do we have one on this initiative?"

Ed answered, "Well, no."

Jane chimed in, "I was kinda wondering the same thing but was afraid to say it, being new and all."

Tim went on, "So, you are telling me that you are trying to create a new software that integrates all your previous twenty years of experience and forty-plus existing software programs to give the industry a new standard of analytics that will separate you from the others in the market, and you are doing so without a project manager? How many people are working on this and how many departments does it touch?"

Joe answered, "This one touches all departments in one way or another and I believe we have well over 20 key people already contributing. But we are late."

"How late?" asks Tim.

"We wanted to go live a year ago, yet are still nowhere close." Joe replied.

"And you have no SPA or 'project manger' leading the project?" Tim added, clearly surprised and masking a statement with a question.

"Umm, correct." Joe responded. He then continued, "SPA?"

Tim said, "Yes, it stands for *Single Point of Accountability.*

Joe answered, "Oh, no, we do not." (See Chapter 8, p. 128, and SPA for Initiatives, p. 129.)

"Well, that is the first place I would start," Tim said, "and I would at the same time get clear on your business goals, so you can align your organization and get people clear about what the right things to work on are. Once you do that, you may have some serious resource conversations to work through. As you get clear about your goals, you may find that you are not prepared to reach them without, at least, some minor tweaks. What do you think? Shall I continue about goals?" asked Tim.

The mood was somber in the room. Both Joe and Ed looked a bit shell shocked, and Jane was not much better. After a long pause Joe spoke up "OK, Tim, I think I am with you but am not sure what I am wading into here. Let's go through this and I will get a better feel."

"OK." Tim then looked at both Jane and Ed and they just sort of nodded, "Here we go." With that Tim went to the whiteboard wrote the words BOTTOM LINE. He then drew a rainbow up from there.

"Oh great," Ed said. "Now we are going over the rainbow!"

"Not exactly," chimed Tim, "but, with clarity, you can go on a great journey!" From there he started explaining bottom-line goals (BLGs) and work processes, and their connection to results.

◊◊◊

Read Chapter Two

CHAPTER 2

Goals

Scenario 1—

Plant Manager 1: "We are currently losing money in the market, it costs us $1.48 per pound to make aluminum ingots and we sell them for $1.36 per pound. If we do not lower the cost of making ingots, we are in trouble as a business. In nine months, our goal is to reduce the cost of producing a pound of ingots to $1.21."

Scenario 2—

Plant Manager 2: "We are not doing so well, we have to improve."

Consultant: "What business metrics are you working towards?

Plant Manager 2: "Metrics? Hmm, not really sure"

The fundamental task of business leadership is to align employees in the same direction. Workplace goals represent that direction. Effective goals are clear, simple, numeric, and measurable. The ability to set simple numeric measurements is an important step in organization alignment. By setting these measurements you give your employees an easier way to see how what they do contributes to the greater good of the organization. This, in turn, helps them to more fully participate in workplace improvements. Without such clarity they are more likely to be reduced to people doing tasks disconnected from the purpose and mission of the organization.

Clarity of goals includes the *bottom line* in each workplace, work group, or department, the *work processes* to be improved, and the *human behaviors* (human factor goals) which must change in order to reach those goals. Clarity also includes *major initiatives or projects* which must be successfully accomplished in order to hit the bottom-line goals.

The majority of managers I've met were, unfortunately, closer to the plant manager in scenario 2. In fact, the two scenarios above are based on real people: plant manager 1 exceeded his goals. Clarity of goals was just one of the reasons he did so, but can you imagine him being successful if he just would have said, "We have to do better"?

The difference between clear goals and no goals is obvious, but the continuum is between no and way-too-many goals. Somewhere in-between lies the sweet spot for every business. Although having too many goals is rare, I worked in one business where they told me they have 172 KPI's (Key Performance Indicators). Since there is a wide continuum, art and science are involved in developing workplace goals. The art lies in the ability to find the right goals and the right number of goals on which to focus in order to meet your overall bottom-line objectives. The science lies in the defining and tracking of the goals.

What Is a Goal?

Developing workplace goals may sound easy but it is a challenge for many. It is common that people do not know their goals and do not even understand what a goal is. Many create actions or lists of tasks and think they are goals. In fact, the distinction between an action, a standard, and a goal is often confused.

Here is a quick way to think about it with an example coming from sales.

An action—Create a service standard for customer requests.

A standard—Reply to customer requests within one hour.

A goal—Reach customer request service standard 95 percent of the time.

Use this analysis to revisit your goals and determine if indeed they are actions or standards. Then sharpen your goals and decide how to best track them.

To improve results, focus on these three goal-related areas: *bottom-line goals*, *work processes*, and *human factors*. Beyond those three major categories, it is common for any workplace to have a certain number of *initiatives* and/or *major projects* that also should be vetted to ensure that they link to the strategic objectives and are properly resourced.

Types of Workplace Goals

Robert Crosby created the following model with Don Simonic at Alcoa. Simonic saw beyond bottom-line goals to the work processes that needed to be improved in order to reach them. He then went one step further and connected the employees, thus creating human factors.

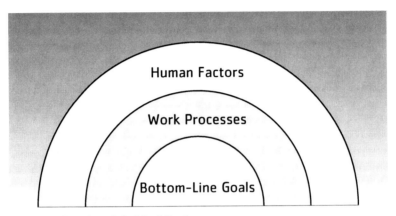

Figure 1 Rainbow Model of Goals

Bottom-Line Goals

Bottom-Line Goals are the reason each area, department, or workplace exists (for sales, it is a specific revenue number). Most businesses set goals each year only at the bottom line . . . X revenue, X Safety, X Production, X Inventory, etc. This may work at a corporate level but to focus the business on how to actually reach the bottom line, you must include two other categories. The first is Work Processes (WPs).

Work Processes

Since BLGs are the reason you exist (for sales, it is a specific revenue number), WPs are how the work flows through each area. In other words, WPs are your task *inputs*, *throughputs*, and *outputs*. The category of Work Processes is critical because identifying the processes that run the business and improving them have a direct impact on the bottom line. In the example used to start this chapter, that same manager started with his bottom-line goal and held sessions where the employees themselves identified and developed which work processes were keeping them from reaching that goal.

Work process improvement requires at least a strategy and perhaps a strategy coupled with a measurable goal. Since some items are harder to measure, such as reducing iterations of reports on quality audits or making sure materials are always on time when there are hundreds of materials on the manufacturing floor, often putting in place a work process improvement strategy is sufficient as long as it is well known and given ample focus to improve. Measure it if you can and create a goal, but if measuring takes too much time and effort, then stay focused on improvement. Clearly, some things still need measurable goals to better understand the problem. Deciding which work processes to improve and whether or not to measure them is where the art of managing comes in.

Focus on work process improvement is key to creating an engaged work-place. All employees know problems with the processes they use on a day-to-day basis to complete their task. Engage your employees to improve them and you will change the dynamics within your workplace. Do it consistently and you will win their hearts and minds and, all the while, improve the bottom line.

All areas have work processes, yet most overlook opportunities to drive behavior change by setting specific measurable goals for the critical processes and then tracking improvement.

Outcome Goals versus Work Processes

Bottom-line goals are about outcomes, amount of sales, amount of production, on time shipments, are all examples. In contrast, work processes concern *how* processes lead to the outcomes: number of quotes, order accuracy, and hit rate of quotes. Workplaces need a balance of both focus areas. All work groups should know their bottom-line goals and, depending on your organizational position, a few work processes to improve in order to get there.

Human Factors

The final area of focus is Human Factors (HFs). Businesses are constantly changing. HFs are strategies put in place to engage your employees in workplace improvement: in other words, processes or methods you use to engage your employees in continuously improving work processes and bottom-line goals. HFs range from problem-solving methods around a specific cross-functional problem, or intact work group development processes. They may include training needs or role and decision clarity. Engaging employees to solve business problems must not be left up to chance. Keeping up with the human side of business is a performance need that must be worked on year-in and year-out. Stop working on it and you will fall behind. Human factor strategies can also include basic trainings, clarity of help chains, role clarity, and higher-level skills such as effective conflict resolution.

Figuring out how to identify and focus on your bottom-line goals is a challenge worth taking. Once you are clear about goals and strategies, then the actions to improve the workplace become much easier. Until you discover the actual goals you need to achieve in your workplace, based on the real situation you are in, you will be feeling in the dark, hoping that you are doing the right thing.

Do you know which work processes are causing you trouble?

If yes, have you set clear goals for each in order to improve them?

If not, how can you identify them?

Do you know how to involve your employees in significant ways to improve your work processes and bottom line?

If not, how can you learn?

These three categories are in a symbiotic relationship. Human factors should support your work processes. Work processes should directly improve your bottom-line goals. When you engage your employees in the right way they will be able to improve the work processes. When you reach or exceed the work process goals–assuming you choose the "right" ones–so also will you achieve or exceed your bottom-line goals.

Each area has the potential for dozens of human factors and work processes but, to be effective, you can only choose the number you can tackle with the resources that you have. Business-critical bottom-line goals tend to be easier to identify, whereas work processes and human factors represent the art of managing. But every department and work team has work processes and human factors that must be tracked in order for effective work to be maintained. Each organizational level has a different responsibility to uphold for the business as a whole to succeed. Those in the executive level must do their tasks, working towards their goals, just as those at each level of leadership and work group.

Finite Resources and Priorities

All workplaces have a finite number of resources. Some, of course, have more resources than others. Yet resource constraints are a reality all must face. Therefore, goal clarity is key to setting priorities. When you combine clear goals with your major projects and/or initiatives you find your real resource constraints. Lack of such clarity results in resources working on things that may or may not be mission critical. Once you align to your goals from the top to the bottom of your organization, then you will be able to make informed choices to better address the real needs of your organization.

Alignment to goals takes strong leadership because it requires time, patience, and a lot of communication. Ensuring goal alignment is critical in order to make sure that you are utilizing the finite number of resources you have on the right things. Goals need to be aligned in each intact work group. The process, if done well, will not only clarify priorities but will help your whole organization learn and improve (see p. 37 of this chapter on Goal Alignment).

It is very dangerous to leave the decision about whether or not to have a conversation to clarify goals up to each work group. Given the choice, many managers would rather just limit their employees' focus to the task-at-hand. Without such a conversation, employees will not learn about the real priorities and managers will not learn from their employees about the little things that could make or break reaching these goals. The former is more likely than the latter. Because of these dimensions, some of your employees may be working on things that do not really matter much in the big picture. Additionally, managers who are not educated by their employees may undervalue some small things that make a big difference in the long run and, inadvertently, lead their employees in a different direction.

The Importance of Balance

Make sure that the goals you create are balanced and complementary. If you set a goal to increase production, it will not help you much unless you also have a goal to improve or at least maintain quality.

Which Goals Are Appropriate for Which Level?

Since each level of the organization has a different focus, it follows that different types of goals are appropriate for each level. Since those higher in the organization do less process work, it is not necessarily needed to create work process goals at the CEO level.

CEO-Level Goals

"Every organization needs a focal point to rally everyone around. Most are not very clear about what is really important; developing a written set of key focus areas and the associated metrics provides this clarity. It also serves to keep people focused over time. By coming back to these critical few things in ongoing reviews and meetings, it serves as a constant reminder about what is truly important. Without this, people will start to substitute their own priorities or, worse yet, become focused on actions and not results."

—Brian Bauerbach
CEO Mold Rite Plastics

Sales	Customer Service
Orders booked	Delivery performance as promised
Net sales	Days late to promise date
A/R days sales outstanding	Lead time
Dollars quoted	Customer complaint rate
Value add margin %	Customer claim dollars
Value add dollars	
Financial	**Manufacturing**
Ebitda: Earnings before interest,	Conversion cost/1,000
taxes, depreciation, amortization	Labor cost/1,000
Ebitda % of sales that is profit	Manufacturing cost/1,000
SGA: Expense selling, general	Inventory dollars
administration cost	Inventory days
SGA divided by volume of sales	Labor hours worked
Cash for additional debt reduction	Production per labor hour
A/P days to pay	Production volume
Capital spending as % of profit	Maintenance supply spending
People	**Safety**
Employee turnover	OSHA recordable rate
Number of employees	Lost work day rate
Percent overtime	

Figure 2 Example CEO Level Goals

The example above is one CEO's list of measures to track. Although the list is not exhaustive, it is a good representation of a manager list to follow and one that gives a broad view. At the CEO and leadership team level of a medium to large organization, the view needs to be both broad and holistic. You must look at many facets and make strategic decisions to position your business for success. Hence, the large number of things to measure as indicated on the previous page. Note that at the CEO level there will be a combination of output goals and process goals, yet they are not tracking the work processes per se.

Additionally, at this level of the organization you may set broad human factor strategies to increase your employees' ability to engage effectively. If your business culture is struggling and you do not set strategies from the highest level, that include yourself and your lead team, then you will leave it up to chance.

Department Goals

Depending on the size of the company you work for, these goals may be much like the CEO-level goals. Yet, if you are a small plant of 200 people or less, your department goals may take on more of a work group feel. You must set clear bottom-line goals, and clear work process and human-factor goals and strategies. And you may or may not have specific projects or initiatives.

Work Team Goals

At the work team level, goal setting is quite clear. Set a bottom-line goal, set the right amount of work process goals, and set complementary human-factor strategies. HF's and WP's may emerge over time through conversations or as it becomes obvious you must improve a facet of your work group.

How Many Goals Are Appropriate?

Now we are back into the art of managing. As I mentioned earlier: "The difference between clear goals and no goals is obvious, but the continuum is between no and way-too-many goals. Somewhere in-between lies the sweet spot for every business. Although having too many goals is rare, I worked in one business where they told me they have 172 KPI's (Key Performance Indicators). Since there is a wide continuum, art and science are involved in developing workplace goals. The art lies in the ability to find the right goals and the right number of goals on which to focus in order to meet your overall bottom-line objectives. The science lies in the defining and tracking of the goals."

All work groups need clear goals, but how many? Which ones are best for each situation? Those questions are best answered by each individual manager. What I can suggest is that you start with one or two bottom-line goals, two or three work process goals, and one or two human factor strategies. The larger your company and the higher you rise, your goals must be broad enough to keep pace with the whole organization.

Goals have a lot of science and some art.

Major Projects and Initiatives

Projects and initiatives are critical to get right. If it is important enough to do, then it is important enough to set clear metrics. All projects must have a *set of specific goals* with the addition of having a *clear timeline* in which they need to be achieved. The simple way of saying it is *what are you trying to achieve* and *by-when?*

We will produce a 26 mm bottle cap, at a low weight (clearly specified) by September of this year. We will produce a capping machine for a specific type of bottle, that will run at a higher speed, by February of next year.

Why do you need a completion date? There are a few reasons. One, a completion date forces real conversations about resources. Two, most projects in competitive markets are intended to help get an edge on your competition or fill a gap in your customers' experience; a completion date then is important to maintain or gain business. Finally, the act of setting a completion date is an act of making a commitment. No completion date equals no commitment.

In fact, for major projects or initiatives there is a definable list of task components to put in place in addition to the goals, at a minimum, to

Write here the project goals, major milestones, and the completion date.	Check task component items not yet effectively in place
_____	☐ Initiating Sponsor (Effectively Sponsoring)
_____	☐ SPA (Project Manager)
_____	☐ Sustaining Sponsors (Effectively Sponsoring)
_____	☐ Decision-Matrix
_____	☐ Visual Timeline Posted (SPA, What, By-When for each task)
_____	☐ Plans for follow through sessions
_____	☐ Kick-off (To clarify this list to organization)

Figure 3 Goal/Task Components Project Work Sheet

help ensure success. Figure 3 represents that list, it is slightly modified from Robert Crosby's book *The Cross-Functional Workplace*.

Note — On this list, I have written "(Effectively Sponsoring)," since you do not "put" Sponsors in place; they already exist. Most miss this critical distinction. The task is to align and build sponsorship once you identify who the actual sponsors are. The sponsor of the work may or may not be sponsoring it effectively (see Chapter 11, p. 177).

Software Development Goals

Director of Engineering: "I want you to know that with the resources we have and the requirements and quality that you are asking for, I can complete this project by October of next year."

Senior Manager: "What? We need it done by February!"

Director of Engineering: "OK, get me more resources and I can do it, or change some of the requirements."

Senior Manager: "But the requirements are set."

Director of Engineering: "Hmm. Well, that only leaves resources?"

Senior Manager: "Wow. No one has ever talked to me about these dynamics before."

Director of Engineering: "Really? How often have you delivered your products on time and to the right specs?"

Senior Manager: "Well . . . Actually, we are always late and often missing some key parts."

Director of Engineering: "I was beginning to guess that. Look, I want to be honest and deliver what I say, when I say I will."

Senior Manager: "That sounds great, but difficult."

Software projects can miss their mark for many reasons. First, the alignment issues dealt with throughout this book happen in all types of workplaces; lack of clarity of priorities and goals are common-place. As you will see later in my chapter on SATA workplace examples, many large initiatives are running in software firms which are not very well aligned. Second, since software is a virtual world, defining the requirements becomes even more critical. In a virtual world, whatever you can imagine you can do; so, if you do not set limits, you may lose control fast. Finally, unrealistic resourcing based on the first two leaves many thinking they will meet deadlines not well thought-out.

The following is a software model intended to help you determine the real needs of any given project.

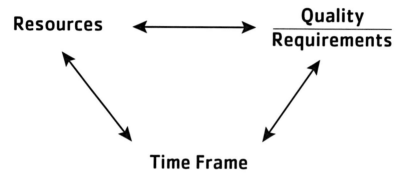

Figure 4 The Triangle Model

The Time Frame

The time frame is self-explanatory. It is simply the date on which you want to ship the software product. In other words, when you want the project done.

Quality and Requirements

Several inter-related issues follow.

Quality. In the software industry this is about how well you de-bug the system. Quality here is about how much risk there is of the product crashing or a feature not working correctly.

Level 1. A website. If a website crashes, very little damage will be done unless it is the primary means of doing business. My company's website could crash, yet it would cause very little damage to our business. In contrast, if Amazon's website crashed for an extended period of time, they would suffer a huge economic blow.

Level 2. Software to run a business: commonly called an ERP system, yet it could be any variety of systems necessary for organizational functioning. If this system goes down it could cost a large company a lot of money. It could be hundreds of thousands or even millions.

Level 3. A defibrillator. If the software used to run a defibrillator crashes, someone might die.

To a great degree, the quality of your product should depend on how well it solves customer needs.

Requirements. These are the software specifications guiding the engineers' efforts. The more complex the requirements are, the longer it takes to create and effectively de-bug the software.

Resources

All development firms have a finite number of resources. Their availability and efficiency dictate the speed at which you can create your software.

The triangle model is intended to help plan effectively by pointing out the levers that exist within a software development project. Once you set any of the points on the triangle model, you narrow your options for affecting the project. For example, if the ship date is set (time frame), you only have Features/Quality or resources that a manager can use as levers to achieve your business goals. A common misconception is to believe that you can keep all three points of the triangle unchanged and yet, inspire or encourage your work group to correct a slipping "ship" date or missed milestones.

Project corrections require a return to goal setting with a pragmatic look at the three options articulated in the Triangle Model. If you want to keep the same requirements and quality standards, then your lever is to add resources. Most high-level managers, in any business, hate that solution. The problem is that if you do not add resources, reduce quality, or simplify requirements you will extend your timeline.

This book is about such conversations, then making real sacrifices to get the product completed on time and with the appropriate level of quality so your customers are fully satisfied. The conversation on page 31 was the beginning of an honest discussion about actual constraints facing the business. In contrast, an unaware workplace *will not* have the difficult conversations, keep working onward, and will keep missing deadlines.

The software industry has moved to different models which play with requirements and quality as well as with ship dates. From *Waterfall* to *Agile* (originally called *Spiral*) to an integrated model that involves things called *Tribes, Squads, Chapters,* and *Guilds;* all are methods attempting to solve the triangle in new ways. Subscription services incorporate this because the product gets multiple updates; therefore, products "ship" much more frequently than in the past. From yearly, to monthly, to weekly and, when trying to fix multiple bugs, sometimes daily.

Aligning Projects and Initiatives

Most workplaces have an abundance of ideas and potential improvements that employees want to work on. If you are not careful, the number of extra initiatives will get out of control, to the point where nobody has any extra time and many initiatives are not getting completed. The best managers understand this and have a way of both tracking the extra initiatives as well as managing them. By "managing them," I mean having the right conversations to determine what should be done now and what can be delayed or stopped altogether. The vetting process in determining what projects or initiatives to work on should include circling back to your bottom-line goals to ensure you are working on the items that will help your current situation and position yourself in the marketplace.

In one situation, a business I worked with listed all their projects and initiatives. It turned out they had 38 initiatives and key projects that were taxing their resources, many of which they were unaware. The leaders then worked a process to talk about and clarify each, reducing the number to fewer than 20, only keeping those deemed "mission critical" to their goals.

High-level leaders beware! Due to your organizational position, when you wander the halls people may think that your thoughts are suggestions and start working on them. This is not a call to stay in your office. Leaders must stay in touch with their work force, yet it is a call to be aware of this dynamic and take precautions to make sure you send a clear message.

A note about initiatives - Be careful when creating initiatives that you are clear about what problem you are trying to solve. Many create solutions or sets of actions that are hard to quantify because they did not exercise due diligence as to what problem they are trying to solve. The problem statement reads as an action or standard (see p. 22) and there is no quantifiable goal. Therefore, they act and say that they have completed a project or initiative, yet they may have not really solved anything.

Go back to page 22 of this chapter and check to see if your initiative is a clear goal. Is it an action, a standard, or a work process goal? If so, then what problem are you trying to solve at a higher level? Take any work process goal and get it as close to a bottom-line goal as possible, if appropriate. Problem-solving goals, like for lean's Kaizen events, may remain at the work process level. One example coming from the manufacturing world is changeovers. The goal is to reduce time to move from producing different colors or different products in half. The clearer you are about what problem you are trying to solve, the easier it will be to gain organization alignment to solve it.

The Importance of Understanding "The Big Picture"

"The Big Picture" is the larger situation you face in the marketplace: the current market conditions, how effectively your organization is doing in that market, and, most importantly, what areas you must improve in order to gain better market position. Do you understand where your business stands in relationship to its competitors? Most employees do not, yet that very information is often driving decisions at the top which impact the employees at all levels.

I am often surprised in difficult moments how rare it is that workplaces share the actual situations they face. Instead, they tend to try topdown short-sighted emergency measures that demoralize the employees and mostly fail because they are conducted too far from the people who really know the possible solutions which would work much better.

Kurt Lewin, talking about the WWII war with Japan, stated: *"In such a situation no special effort is required to keep morale high. The very combination of a definitive objective, the belief in final success and the realistic facing of great difficulties is high morale. The individual who makes extreme efforts* *and accepts great risks for worth-while goals does not feel that he is making a sacrifice, instead he merely feels that he is acting naturally."*

OK, so most companies are not fighting a war, yet in today's workplace there are many dire scenarios of which the employees are unaware; the leaders have not shared the real pain they are in. How many plants have you heard about which were suddenly closed and moved to a new location in order to produce the product more cheaply? Imagine how hard the workers would work if they knew the scenario they were in and the production improvements they needed to achieve to keep the plant in place. Add in the mix solid problem-solving and workplace-improvement strategies and likelihood of success gets even greater.

In dire circumstances, just sharing the situation is not enough. You need to also have a plan, complete with a solid structure, and process to involve employees in helping solve the issues. To do that, you need the organization alignment this book advocates. With such a strategy you can involve those closest to the work and not only reach unthinkable business numbers, but also increase morale along the way. Cost cutting and increasing production are a few of the areas that can most easily be achieved with a combination of honesty and an effective people strategy to solve the problems.

On the flip side, I have seen business after business solve their yearly cost problems or production issues by making decisions from on high and imposing them below. In each scenario, businesses who maintained the pattern each year slowly self-destructed into layoffs, early retirements, and significant loss of market share.

Tracking As a Form of Listening

"I have found that the act of tracking items and setting goals around that tracking is a deep form of listening. Most think they don't have the time to do so. *Yet, if you spend the time to listen by tracking what is going on, you will save a lot of time.*"

—John Nicol
Partner and General Manager, Microsoft

I have worked with many people who said they were having problems and were not actually tracking the areas where they were struggling. In most of those cases, just by tracking the items they were concerned with the obvious problems emerged and the organizations were able to solve their issues.

John Nicol talked about taking over a division that had developed set-top boxes providing consumers with Internet access. On hearing reports that customers were upset by lack of service, he was unclear of the cause or extent of the problem. His first act was to track all devices by pinging them, then noting their location on a US map. He prominently positioned a large LCD monitor, so the engineers could see the real-time problem and track progress. The first thing they learned was that a whole area of the southeast had poor service or even no service. The very act of tracking gave them data to confirm the magnitude of the issue; from there they put in place measures that ensured all customers were on-line.

In a similar experience at a print shop having problems with late shipments, I asked: "How many are late?"

The manager replied: "I am not sure." So, I asked him to start tracking each job and recording each late shipment and its cause(s). He did so by using a large whiteboard and displaying it prominently to visually track all the print jobs so that all the employees could easily see them. This simple act of tracking and providing a feedback loop to the workplace quickly led to discovering little issues that were solvable and within a few weeks they had reduced the late shipments to less than 5 percent of all orders. Not all situations are quite so simple, yet surely there are many where simple tracking can aid learning and quick workplace improvements.

Goal Alignment

Setting goals can add excitement and challenge to your workplace. For many however, it is just another mundane task. Once you use your goals to align your workplace they will take on new meaning and energy. I started this chapter by saying: "The fundamental task of leadership is to align their employees in the same direction. Workplace goals represent that direction." Therefore, just setting clear goals is not enough. You must use those goals to *align* and *engage* your work force in order to translate the direction to results! Since there are finite resources in all workplaces, aligning them to successfully reach your goals represents a challenge that is worthy of engaging all employees to help solve. Don't miss this opportunity.

Most businesses treat goal setting as an annual event, yet miss the golden opportunity it presents. The most common practice is to set next year's goals X percent higher than last and then move on to "real work," no matter how clear or fuzzy the plan. Normally the pressure to "get to work" far outweighs the pressure to "plan and reflect on the work." The opportunity missed is to not only align the employees to the goals, but also to engage them in creating a plan on how to reach them. Engage and align effectively and you create a far greater chance of success. After such an effort, if the business falls short, it is likely because of factors outside of its control–like a global recession!–but major improvements on indexes of cost, quality, productivity, and safety will still be obtained.

Effective goal alignment has some key components and requires time spent "planning the work" despite pressure to get going. It is also an iterative process in which each business can only start wherever they are and move towards clarity. Skip this and the likelihood of incremental sustainable improvements decreases.

Once you have created clear goals, as outlined in this chapter, you are ready for the next steps in the process. Here are the key components.

Use an effective group process and cascade to all major groups – Alignment of goals requires engaging all employees who work to achieve them. That alignment must be done in intact work groups. Clarity and retention is increased through dialogue, a constructive back-and-forth on a topic, rather than through one-way communication. Remember, psychologists say people only retain 30 percent of what they read. Most finish a book only if engaged, yet even then only retain around 30 percent.

Despite this, many give goals through one-way communication which contributes to a passive workplace. Use of an effective group process that involves dialogue, and critical thinking in each intact work group is a key component of successful goal alignment.

Most managers are deficient here. At best, they have read about group process but have little or no formal training. At worst, they were trained in a technical field, excelled in their craft, and are now responsible to manage people and lead groups.

To cascade goal alignment, start with the lead team. Have the manager clarify the corporate goals, share them with the rest of the lead team, and create the location or division's goals. Roll the division goals back up to the corporate manager to verify that they are the right goals to reach the corporate objectives. From here, the task is to dialogue about the goals and have the group suggest work processes which need more focus.

Once that conversation is complete, it is time to dive deeper into the organization. Think of the overall goals as a large pie with each department responsible for their piece. Have all department heads develop their piece which support the division goals in all three categories, (Often, I also have them generate feedback on what they need from the other departments in order to reach their goals.) After that, each department head presents its goals (and feedback) to the whole lead team, then works the data through a dialogue. The top manager must say whether the department is on the right track, with help from the rest of the group, and adjust what each department is working on if needed in order to make sure they are working on the right things to reach the overall goals. Through this process, the lead team will create greater clarity on the goals they are working on, a greater understanding of what all departments are trying to achieve, and what they need from each other to get there. Each department should create approximately 1 to 2 BLGs, 3 to 5 WPs, and 1 to 2 HFs (although there is no magic number).

Next, work with each department and each intact work team to clarify the goals, and have the employees raise the critical issues needed to reach them. Go as far down the organization as you can, remembering that hourly employees are very knowledgeable about the best way to achieve results. Warning! Bosses must still decide on priorities and follow up robustly. Failure to follow up could have the unintended consequence of slighting those who have given ideas. If you do not follow up well, do not blame the employees for being skeptical the next time you ask for input.

Connecting Task to Big Picture. If done well, all employees should understand how their task fits into their department's goals, how those in turn fit into the division or location's and, ultimately, the corporation's goals. *Imagine the power of having all your employees understand how their tasks help the business reach its overall goals!*

See across the whole system – Here are a few things to look for.

Victim thinking – for example, "I have always gotten bad information from X (any department); that is just the way it is." It is easy to get used to the status quo; and departments often get stuck in their silos. It does not have to be that way, however. Strategies can be created to solve problems of missing data from any department and begin to reduce errors. Each person who does not take appropriate responsibility for accurate inputs and information is helping to maintain the status quo.

Work process goals out of whack – There is a tendency for each department to focus on the bad or missing stuff from every other department and to not put appropriate WPs in place, needed to drive improvements from their own employees. This is really another form of victim thinking. If a facilitator listens to the problems of each group, obvious gaps in focus will appear; these need to be addressed. Sales may forget to take steps to reduce order errors; production may forget to focus on critical process errors; and engineering may forget to focus on Bill of Materials accuracy. The goal is to have each intact group and department take full responsibility for their own areas as well as understand the interconnectedness of the workplace.

Follow this with a session where all department managers gather to further see across the whole system. In this session, share learnings, derive implications, and build further strategies for improvement.

Be diligent – It is easy to let a people process get away from you. A process like this will allow you to learn and understand all the issues in your workplace. It is easy to leave with a huge laundry list and only accomplish some of it. Finish off the first go-round with honest conversations about how much work the list really requires and what you will and will not work on based on your current resource realities, needs, and priorities. The lead team must make decisions and justify, through both financial numbers and potential morale implications to their workforce, what to work on. This becomes even more critical if it is obvious that the list got larger than available resources can achieve. Part of the decision process has to be to notice items that seem little but that can make or break what gets done.

This is the work and responsibility of the lead team. Refining what will be worked on is best done in dialogue with the location manager and the rest of the staff. Stretch yourself but also be realistic. Ultimately, your department may have to work on some things that you do not deem important. Equally important is communicating with your group about which items get taken off the list and why. Most employees can live with decisions that they disagree with, if they at least understand why.

Finally, you must follow up this work (see Chapter 10: Follow-Up). Within a few months, spend the time to bring all groups back together to take a look and make course corrections. Leaving goal alignment up to checking off a list at the end of the year misses the mark. Remember the pressure to "get to work" far outweighs the pressure to "plan the work" in most organizations. Do not let that stop you from having people pause for a few hours and continue planning the work. The follow-up must go beyond 'did you do the task' to dialogue about whether you are getting the intended results. After all, these tasks were just the best guess at what would solve the problem. Even if they were done well, the problem may not be solved. The cost of not doing follow-up in both real dollars and organizational momentum is too great to let it slide.

Goal alignment gives every business a golden opportunity. Seize it with an effective group process and create a clear and unified path towards business results!

Once you clarify your goals, then your employees will have tangible items around which to align. The next step of organization alignment is a theory that is perhaps the most critical in order to do this, called "Sponsor Agent Target Advocate." Chapters 3, 5, 6, and 11 are specifically devoted to SATA, which informs this entire book.

The Conversation Continues

About an hour later, Joe looked confused, a bit frustrated, yet also a bit perky. "Tim," he said, "I have a take on why goals matter, but I would like to hear why you think clarifying goals is critical."

"Sure," responded Tim. "If you don't clarify goals and the work processes that need to be improved to reach them, as well as decide on what major initiatives and projects you will complete, then your employees will have a harder time knowing what and why they are doing their tasks, and won't as easily be able to recognize or engage in needed improvements.

Also, each initiative and project have specific managers at different levels who must keep their priorities and resources focused or they will not accomplish the tasks needed to successfully complete them."

Tim paused to catch his breath, but looked quite energized and passionate.

"If you just leave things at a fuzzy high level, then employees will do what they 'think' is important or will begin to fight others for resources. Essentially, they will advocate, consciously or not, for what they think is best, versus what has been methodically thought through at a high level, researched in the marketplace, and talked about down through the organization to see what you need to achieve in order to be successful."

Tim almost seemed somber as he continued now.

"Organizations should align around their bottom-line goals. *Don't align because its a good idea; align to your goals to focus your work team and get your resources working on the right stuff* so you can accomplish them and have an idea of whether or not you are actually resourced correctly."

"I am often surprised at managers and, employees charged with helping drive change, who do not seem to know the distinctions I talk about in my chapter on goals. They do not know the distinction of *What is a goal; What is a standard; What is an action; What is a problem; What is a solution*; nor how to engage the right people from a systemic perspective to create clarity and alignment around those distinctions.

If you don't spend the time to align your organization to its goals, and you need to spend the time from work group to work group, **then you will only be guessing** and miss out on the difficult generative conversations around alignment that create clarity and solidify direction.

The reality is that in most organizations employees want to pretend that there are no conflicts and that everything is OK when it is often not. Difficult conversations need to happen or you will not reach your business objectives.

Sorry, Joe, I got a little emotional," Tim said. "But I am often shocked and surprised by what I see and hear happening in most organizations. Aligning goals is a pay-now or pay-later affair; most seem to think they can just get to work and all will be fine. Sadly, that means they opt to pay later."

Tim, looking clear-eyed and straightforward, added, "Of course, Joe, all scenarios are different. If your projects and initiatives have been completed on time and you have been reaching your business objectives then going work group by work group is not that important. You have to ask yourself: what has been the scenario and how well have we been accomplishing our tasks?"

Joe spoke up, "No need to apologize, Tim. I like your passion. I also can see that I have really been skipping some critical conversations that could take the work many places. I will avoid those conversations no longer. Although, I must admit, they are not my favorite." Joe looked excited yet a little skittish.

He continued, "I have really missed the boat on resources. *I just went with the philosophy that smart people could just figure it out. I can see the problems that creates as even smart people need coordination from their boss.* OK, I am ready to get back to the office to work on this stuff!" "Joe, before you go, I think it would be wise to have another conversation, plus I need to talk to you all about the next critical theory that aids alignment," Tim said looking a bit nervous.

Ed had already stood up and looked surprised, "What conversation is that? And what, another theory?"

Tim continued, "Yes, the theory is about how to fully understand and align your system. But the conversation that I strongly suggest we tackle today is about a key resource decision. I suggest that you decide today or very soon, who the project manager is on the Smart project. Having no defined project manager on an initiative this important seems less than wise to me."

"But, Tim," Ed spoke up, "we often let groups manage things."

"Yes, Ed, I understand," said Tim, "but it sounds like that has not worked and, by the way, I don't think it really ever does. So, I am suggesting a new way to gain clarity and direction."

"Boy, I fear that people won't like this." Ed stated, looking perplexed.

"Me, too," said Joe, "Yet I cannot see how we can go on the same way. Too often, everybody wants to be in-the-know about all things, and often many of those asking really do not need the info. Yet, in contrast, I spend too little time in dialogue with the people who need absolute clarity about direction. I can see how my actions have allowed the workplace to take on more of a life of its own than is necessary. I wonder if we have a trust issue in our organization. To me, this one has to change even if, at first, people don't like it."

"Wise words," said Tim. "Often a sign of low trust is a workplace where there is lack of this type of clarity. But that is just a theory. The reality is that you need one person accountable and bird-dogging all actions on all key initiatives and you need to know the actual status, good or bad news, at any given time."

Tim continued, "That brings us back to the SMART project. Could Jane be your project manager?"

"Me?" Jane chimed in, after watching last few exchanges with fascination.

Ed was first to speak, "Jane is now working on our core product as well as two mission-critical projects. I cannot see how she could do this. Why don't we use one of the regular project managers?"

Joe spoke up, "She's what? Wow, that is a lot all right. Hmm, pity, seems Jane is so tuned into the needs of our customers, as PM she could really ensure the right product."

"Jane, do you have PM experience?" Ed asked.

"Sure I do!" Jane said. "I have my PMP certificate and led many projects in my last job. My concern is bandwidth."

Tim spoke, "Joe and Ed, your task here is to be honest about the time it takes for quality work to be done and decide who is the right project manager. If you go on the same way, with no change in resources or structure yet expecting a different outcome, I predict you will fail."

"Ed," Joe asked, "What is stopping us from putting Jane on this?"

Ed replied, "Well, there is a lot of pressure to maintain our core platform and Jane needs to get involved but, to be honest, we probably have more resources that could support our core product than could create such a specialized project as SMART."

Joe took a second to reflect, then responded back, "Ed, I am ready to put Jane on this project right now and take away all her other duties, unless you can convince me otherwise."

Ed, clearly energized, responded immediately, "OK! Let's do this!"

"Wow," Jane remarked. "Sounds like my life just got simpler and more complicated, all in matter of a few seconds!"

Laughter broke out, a burden lightened.

Tim spoke up, "OK, the next step is to fully understand your system, and the roles that are there. In fact, the roles you are about to learn are in all systems: everywhere. For success in a project that is important and new to your business, these roles need to be identified, educated, and prepped for the upcoming work in order to fully align to this project."

Tim then went to his whiteboard and began to sketch out a theory that seemed foreign to Ed, Joe, and Jane, yet it somehow made sense and began to help in an odd way. Then he said, "How about if we meet again in a week and build a strategy to move forward?"

Joe, Jane, and Ed looked at each other and Joe said, "Sounds great."

Jane noticed herself relaxing: the first time in two weeks. It seemed her CEO and boss were using what they are learning in a remarkable ways.

◊◊◊

Read Chapter Three

CHAPTER 3

Sponsor/Agent/Target/ Advocate

Scenario 1 —

Employee: "You just don't understand. To get projects completed around here, I have to beg for resources and outmaneuver fellow workers. Even if I am successful, most projects are late and over budget. We all have too much work."

Consultant: "Wow, it must be hard to do your work. I am confident that once you gain proper Sponsorship for your projects, your work will become easier and more productive. Understanding and applying SATA is the key!"

Scenario 2 —

Lead team participant: "I have had many meetings like this, but this is the first time that at the end we really owned the results!"

Both scenarios above are real. The first highlights common problems in misaligned organizations. The second occurred after an executive lead-team meeting I facilitated. During that meeting, I continuously raised awareness of the various aspects of organization theory and, most importantly, carefully stayed within my role of a Change Agent as defined by Sponsor/Agent/Target/Advocate (SATA). It is at the core of all my work. The theory of SATA was first articulated in 1991 by Daryl Conner and has gained further clarity in the ensuing years. I see it more as a reality than a theory. It is a critical component of system alignment and employee empowerment.

SATA is a tool to analyze the interactions between key organization roles, each with a critical function, who may be either performing effectively or under- or over-functioning. The roles themselves are definitional, meaning that you are in them at each moment whether you realize it or not. *Sometimes you are in multiple roles at the same time.*

SATA is not a top-down theory; it is a map of legitimate authority. There are several moments when using SATA is critical; one of the most common is when you are unable to complete a task because another key person is not cooperating. The common temptation in these moments is to blame the employee which, whether you are aware of it or not, is an *individual* theory of change. SATA, however, is a *systemic* theory that helps organizations use a wider perspective. SATA holds the key to effective day-to-day work, planning for any size of project or initiative, and as a constant compass if you are in the role of consultant or change agent. Further, the power of SATA is that it is a definitional model that identifies whichever role you are in at any moment. Each role has specific behavioral requirements which must be met to ensure success.

The Four Key Roles:

The Sponsor

Sponsors are the persons with legitimate authority over the employees doing the work. They provide task component clarity when needed, vision or direction usually in the form of goals, consequence management, follow through of work, and resources in the form of time, money, and people. *Since all workplaces have a finite amount of resources, perhaps* **the most critical resource a Sponsor will provide is time** *for the Targets to do their task.* Each work task, initiative, or project always has one or, depending on the number of departments involved, multiple sponsors. Therefore, Sponsors exist on all tasks whether they are aware of it or not.

Sponsors, like other key roles, have a definitional meaning. In other words, no matter what the scenario at work and no matter who you are working with, there is always one Sponsor of the work who either is or is not sponsoring effectively. By definition, the direct boss of whomever you are trying to get work done with IS the Sponsor of that person. Whether they support what you are trying to do is another story.

A note about the word "Sponsor" - The word Sponsor in our–and most–cultures has been used in many ways. Perhaps the most common use of Sponsor is in relation to an event, as in "and now a word from our sponsor." It is often used to support, promote, champion, or finance someone. I have often thought I should find a less confusing word. (Please use whatever word you want. I am sticking to the original language in order to honor Conner, the creator of this theory. This book represents our unique adaptation of his work.)

Two Types of Sponsors

There are two types of Sponsors: Sustaining and Initiating. *The person directly above the person you are interacting with is the **Sustaining** Sponsor.* Sustaining Sponsors, most critical during large-change initiatives and cross-departmental projects, are often neglected. Without their support, employees may not focus on the right tasks, more often out of ignorance than conscious resistance. There are as many sustaining sponsors on a task as there are employees who report to different bosses, as well as layers in between the work and a single sponsor above all people. All Sponsors need to be on-board so they are not inadvertently hurting the effort. The most critical Sustaining Sponsor is whoever is in charge of the people where the work is taking place.

The next type of Sponsor is the Initiating Sponsor. In all large-scale change efforts, if you go up the organizational chart, you will find one person who is over all departments and employees impacted by the change, initiative, or project. By definition, *the **Initiating Sponsor** of any large-scale change, project, or initiative is the single boss over all who have tasks to accomplish, all those impacted, and all who will use day-to-day after the implementation.* Do not be confused by the word "initiating." This does not necessarily mean that they started, or even condoned, the change, project, or initiative, because it is a definitional reality. In fact, many unaware Initiating Sponsors, unintentionally, may assign competing goals, initiatives, or directives. It is not that they need to know about everything. If a change is large or important enough, however, the Initiating Sponsor needs to have enough knowledge to ensure support for it to be successful. The lack of awareness of these two roles causes untold disruption in the form of confusion, delays, and, ultimately, higher costs.

Learn How to Drive Sponsorship

The major task of the Sponsor is to learn how to provide and drive appropriate sponsorship in order to keep the organization focused and moving towards its vision or goals. They do this by learning what is happening throughout the organization: above, below, and sideways. This takes constant communication and persistence.

Additionally, they must provide clear expectations to their employees while fostering an environment where accurate data flows. If you are a sponsor and you get upset at people when they tell you difficult truths, then do not expect them to be forthcoming in the future. Another key to successful sponsoring is keeping an eye on the amount of work you want the organization or your work team to accomplish and having the courage to slow down at times so work gets effectively completed, instead of having too many tasks with little or nothing getting done. Effective sponsorship is a never-ending task. Stop focusing on it and you will not get your desired results.

The Change Agent

Change Agents are the people who help the work or task get completed. Their job is to facilitate the work being done. Change agents are often technical experts in what they do; therefore, their real job is to impart knowledge through education. In fact, *education is a key role of the change agent.* Like the Sponsor, the Change Agent has a definitional role. *Anytime you work outside your department to get something done, you are a **Change Agent.** By definition, if you need something from another whom you have no authority over in order to complete your task, you are also a Change Agent.* If you are an external consultant working inside of any business, you are always a change agent.

Maintenance, safety, HR, and quality all live mainly in the role of change agent. R&D people who need to use a machine on the floor to test product are Change Agents whenever they are trying to use the machine. *The problem for most in the role of Change Agent is that they don't know they are in it.* Believe me, when you go into a department and want to get something, the person you are trying to work with always knows that you have no positional authority over them and that they really don't have to listen to you unless . . . you are sponsored to do so!

As I wrote earlier, education is the key to an effective Change Agent, but, ironically, it is in this area where many miss the mark. The reason is that most are not trained in or even aware of half of their educational responsibilities.

There are two key areas where the Change Agent must continually educate: first, the task *component or technical* aspect of their work which is the reason most Change Agents get their roles, and second, the *systemic* aspect of the project, work, change, or initiative.

The latter is where work tasks most often break down. Change Agents must learn how to build sponsorship for their work. It is simple: *without sponsorship there will be no effective work.* On larger projects this means making sure all sustaining sponsors understand and are updated with upcoming tasks on the current timeline, plus know how to use the structures created for information flow. It also means conversations with the Sponsor(s) to get clear about their expected outcomes, needs, and wants, to get the right people involved with decision points, to help them monitor and adjust resources, and to coach them on *what* to say to their employees and *when*, in order to ensure *alignment, commitment,* and *success.*

If you read the above as a one-time task, then you are misreading what I am saying. *This is constant work and, when done well, the rewards will be significant.* On smaller day-to-day tasks, it is making sure the task is still critical, and keeping up-to-date on the timing needed to execute well. *A Change Agent who learns how to leverage the system and build sponsorship by educating the right people will have great success and never know the meaning of employee resistance.*

The Target

The **Target** *is, by definition, the one who carries out the work.* If you are working with a person who is to provide you information, or a project team member who is responsible for a specific project task and must keep you posted, or someone who is to provide you something from another department, each is a Target. The quality person who tells someone on the floor to scrap product is talking to a Target. The software implementer who is trying to configure a system by talking to an employee, who will eventually use it, is talking to a Target. It again is a definitional term. *Please note - **Targets** are either those doing the work today, or those who will use the product, tool, or service upon implementation.*

In fact, part of the power of SATA is that no matter what you are doing in any organization, all roles exist and you are in at least one of them. Find the roles, and you will clarify how to ensure effective work is done. The Target is often missed entirely and, ironically, is the single-most blamed person for resistance to change. In reality, resistance is often just a Target who knows major problems that aren't being addressed, or that there is a disconnect between what their boss expects them to do, and what the Change Agent in front of them wants. Often, the Change Agent and Target trying to work together do not understand their SATA roles.

Targets play a critical role in getting systems aligned and effective work implemented. First, they must raise all issues that are in the way of success—which, by the way, they always know and are often not asked. This is why so many change efforts fail. *Oops, I forgot to talk to the people actually working where the new process, initiative, software system, etc. will take place.*

Consultant: "So you are creating this to be used by whom?"

Employee (un-SATA aware Change Agent): "Oh, it's a new way to estimate for the people estimating."

Consultant: "Great and when will it be done?"

Employee: "Sometime next month."

Consultant: "Cool, so how have the estimators taken to it?"

Employee: "Oh, they don't know about it yet because I haven't shown them; I did not want to bother them till it is ready to implement."

Consultant (surprised): "Hmm. How about showing it to them when it is about ready, but getting feedback as to whether it works, then adjusting it to ensure it's what they need?"

Employee: "Oh, wow! I never thought of that. OK, I will do a dry run with them in the next few weeks and then adjust the system based on their feedback."

Does the scenario above sound familiar? It is real and happens often in organizations. Targets have the unique knowledge that comes from doing the work. Their knowledge is the most underutilized in organizations. The Target's job is to impart this knowledge to the Change Agent(s) and the Sponsor on a consistent basis. *They must tell what is and isn't working and have structured ways to do this day-to-day regarding all major initiatives.*

The second thing a Target must learn how to do is to help the system get in alignment by not doing tasks that are out of the Target's perceived scope. Instead, they must learn how to use these moments to help gain workplace alignment. Therefore, saying "No" must be part of all Target's vocabulary, yet stopping there is not good enough. They must be willing to say, "No. Sorry, this task is beyond the scope of my work. If you clear it with my boss, however, I am willing and happy to help." Of course, I am not saying: don't be helpful if needed. If you can help and it doesn't disrupt your work, then fine, but if what you are being asked to do threatens the priorities set by your boss, then learn to say no.

Targets need to learn how to identify Change Agents working out of alignment and help leverage their sponsor to get the system back in alignment. Most organizations have stories about initiatives that turned into disasters. Effective targets are always looking to keep the system in alignment. Managers can move fast and are making good faith efforts to get the work done. Most misalignment that happens in business is unintentional. Targets are normally the first ones to recognize when the organization is out of alignment. *To be an effective target is to raise alignment issues so the system gets back on track.* Managers can help by first encouraging this behavior, and then thanking the employees that do it.

A note about the choice of using the word "Target": The meaning of word "target" in our language can confuse the intent of how we are using it. You might even say it often is seen as a harsh or negative word. It is so negative for some companies that they substitute a different word for target. I support that but also want to keep to the original language used by Connor and Crosby. In addition, I have never found a word that fully fits what I want to express. So, with that said, please know that I am using it here to simply identify *who does the work* with no intention of it being anything but descriptive. I support you finding the language that works for you in your own location.

The four key roles of SATA are critical for effective business function-ing, whether it is day-to-day work or major changes. In my 20 years of consulting, I have often heard about people who were problems, but I have yet to talk to any employees who say "they" are the problem. It is my contention that, due to the almost universal misunderstanding of SATA, many well-intentioned people get scapegoated when they were simply just trying to get their work done. Organization alignment is a struggle in every kind of business; it can only be achieved by first committing to SATA-like principles, then through constant communications. Like a marriage: stop working on it, and problems start.

The Advocate

Advocates also have a clear definition. *They are the people who want some-thing different.* This could be a minor change all the way to a major way in which work gets done. While leading sessions, I have often asked people to "raise your hand if you want something different today or have ever wanted anything different at work"; each time the results were the same. All hands went up. Therefore, the advocate can come from any role. A Sponsor who wants a particular change and articulates it to their employ-ees is, by definition, an Advocate. Their task is to first clearly articulate the change and then, begin to drive it. Most Advocates in business, however, are not so lucky. They must go in search of a Sponsor—and not just any Sponsor. It must be the right Sponsor who can actually provide the lever-age to successfully implement the change. Most Advocates are not aware they are Advocates and do not know to whom they should bring their idea. I have been in some organizations where there are bitter people who have wanted change for years, yet have seen no success.

What is an Advocate to Do?

Advocates must identify the Sponsor over the work area where they want change—often it is their direct boss. They must then clearly articulate *what they want, how it is useful, and what the organization will gain* from its implementation. Once you have found the right person and have given it your best effort, prepare yourself for a few possibilities.

First, and the easiest to swallow, is it may be accepted and then the effort of how to do it begins. Or, second, it will be rejected and you now have a much more difficult task. This is so because *once you have been rejected you must give up the fight or risk alienation* and becoming a problem for the organization. Advocates without sponsorship will not get anywhere and, if they remain vocal, may be seen as problems. Those who do not give up risk becoming bitter. Don't blame the organization if that is your fate.

Advocacy is wonderful; all Sponsors should encourage and nurture it. New ideas fuel greater productivity and keep employees alive. Raise awareness of what it is and learn how to use it to your advantage. Without this awareness you risk going down the road of many organizations whose employees experience their ideas not being taken seriously, so they simply stop offering them.

To help clarify each role further, I have created the following charts that show the interrelationship of each SATA role.

Responsibilities of Each SATA Role

Each SATA role has critical systemic responsibilities, whether the person in the role is aware of them or not. When performed well, these roles enable high-level functioning. The following charts highlight: a) linkages of various SATA role and b) important role components. Each chart also illustrates feedback loops. Notice that in all situations they go both ways. In order for effective work to happen, feedback must be a two-way dialogue, no matter which positions are talking to each other in the organization. Listening and learning precede taking action and making adjustments when at all possible.

This is an area where under-functioning persists. When given direction, many employees have concerns that don't get voiced; this has potential to cause their work to suffer. Do they have responsibility to speak up? Of course, but if they speak up and get an angry response, do not expect them to do so next time. Systemic thinking is critical to promote effective workplaces because it looks at the whole rather than the parts, and provides answers to improve the inter-relationships among all parties. Handling difficult information from any level is a key to fostering a safe environment where anything can be said. Absolute clarity comes from dialogue. Leadership and/or effective facilitation is the key to foster such dialogue. There are many ways to structure conversations to promote dialogue including the simple act of gate-keeping. But know, it is a choice that all leaders make whether they are clear about it or not. Taking the victim position "Our people just don't speak up" will allow your work team to continue to miss out on potentially critical information about issues and problems.

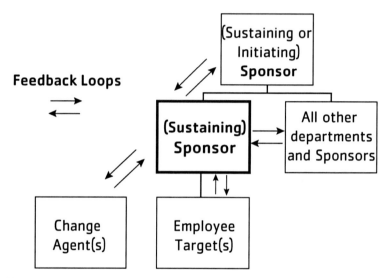

Figure 5 Sponsor Responsibilities

Explanation of Figure 5

From their own Initiating or Sustaining Sponsor: Get clarity of direction, goals, and boundaries. Confirm and adjust any resource needs and raise any issues in the way of success that you need help with or want more visible. Adjust priorities on an as-needed basis.

To the Change Agent(s): Clarify the scope of the work, understand the impact of change, ensure a structure for feedback, and adjust the work to fit bottom line or stop it if unnecessary. Clarify expectations for how the Change Agent and Targets must work together to ensure an effective implementation. Align with all employees or departments who could impact or are impacted by the change or work. Monitor until results are achieved.

To the Target(s): Provide time, tools, goal clarity, and expectations. Give appropriate authority to make fast decisions. Monitor work and drive improvements.

To all other departments and Sponsors: Clarify and ensure input and output needs, and align across departments and functions. Keep track of day-to-day needs and how departments are working together.

Sustaining Sponsors have perhaps the most complicated SATA role in the organization due to their systemic position. They are responsible to manage up, down, and sideways, as well as to pay attention to any person who is interacting within their department. Only CEOs are relieved from managing sideways and up, and even they may have to manage a board, an owner, or an investment firm. The best Sustaining Sponsors are aware of this complexity and maintain clarity of purpose when they interrelate with their peers (side-to-side) and their Sponsor (up).

At each level of the organization, there is a capacity to understand the impact of decisions within that area that is different than that of someone who is looking from on high. Effective Sponsors can help shape top-down decisions due to their clarity of the impact it will have. The best are crystal clear about the bottom line, the nuances of what will negatively or positively impact the bottom line, and are able to cite specifics, if need be, to push back. They are also consistently able to ask for the resources, people, and equipment they need to pursue record numbers. Over- and under-functioning at this level, however, will result in tension or work that suffers between direct reports, between sideways departments, or with the direct boss.

A common area that is missed is linking cross-functional departments that must support each other in order for work to be accomplished. At the *Initiating Sponsor level, under-functioning in the form of unclear expectations and holding departments accountable to work well together* is an epidemic among plant-level leaders and CEOs. Many avoid making people or departments work well with each other. Others go immediately into personal models of behavior, versus thinking systemically, and blame one employee or the other if tension exists, rather than to say, "You must supply resources on time with quality across departments, and you must learn exactly what that means. You don't have to like each other, but you do have to work together. Your departments must support each other to the point that all employees get the materials, support, and information they need 95 to 100 percent of the time without significant waiting."

Of course, just saying that is not enough; you then have to follow up until the plan put in place is obtaining the desired business results.

Today's workplaces cannot afford to waste time on who is right or wrong in these scenarios; they must focus on what each department needs, tweak them until they are correct, and deliver them on time with quality. The Initiating Sponsor above those departments cannot just say, "Work better together" or "You guys figure this out," then walk away. They must stay connected by setting an appropriate date for the parties who are in conflict to bring them a plan for resolution. Then, either put the plan in place or slightly tweak it to fit the circumstances, as well as establish follow-up dates. Further, they must also break any impasses quickly and not allow future conflicts to remain.

Finally, all Sponsors have a responsibility to understand the resources, reporting to other managers, yet are currently working in their department to accomplish specific tasks or perform day-to-day activities. *These people are, by definition, Change Agents.* Of course, having to know each time a person external to your department walks in is too much, but knowledge of mission-critical projects or day-to-day essential activities that your area is getting help with, obviously, is the key to being able to support them. Without this knowledge the Sponsor, at worst, will inadvertently undermine the initiative. At best, the task will get lucky and slide through but will likely have a reduced impact. I have seen huge conflicts between external resources and the employees in a work area when the Sponsor of the work did not even know that people outside of their department were on their shifts and had tasks to perform. Managing the Change Agents on your shift is a critical function of sponsorship. Get aligned with groups that interact within your area, and cross-functional tasks become easier, even if it means that items get stopped or delayed that some of your direct reports think are important. If you blame the problems in your area on other departments then, ironically, the problems will likely remain. From such a complicated position in the system, it is very easy to get into a victim role and start blaming all your woes on others. Take the reins of leadership and you can move mountains!

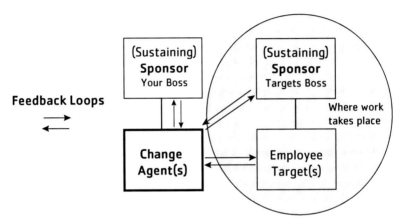

Figure 6 *Change Agent Responsibilities*

Explanation of Figure 6

From their Sustaining Sponsor (their boss): The Change Agent's boss is their Sponsor, but not the Sponsor of the work. *The Change Agent must help the alignment between it's boss and the Sponsor where the work is taking place.* They must pay constant attention to how well or poorly the alignment is or they risk over-functioning. Get clarity of standards, process steps, and boundaries from their boss. With the Sponsor of the work, highlight anything competing with success. Raise resource needs such as tools and time. Raise any issues in the way of succeeding that you need help with or want to raise visibility for. Clarify priorities on an as-needed basis. Create a system to monitor progress.

From the Sustaining Sponsor (Target's Boss): *The boss of the employees where the work takes place is, by definition, the Sponsor of the work.* Understand the impact of the change and scope of work, and create a structure for feedback. Understand the expectations of how to work with the Targets. Raise items that may impede success. Continually educate on the amount of time needed where the work will take place. Create a simple system to monitor until results are achieved.

To the Target(s): Facilitate the change or work. Listen to their concerns and adjust work accordingly. Educate specifics of the task and help facilitate effective working relationships. If a tool is in development, share with the Target(s) early enough so they can give feedback to shape the tool to suit their needs, prior to implementation.

Change Agents also have a dubious task in an organization. They are accountable to a boss who is not over the people whom they are working with. Their success or failure depends on alignment with what they are trying to accomplish. What they most often miss, however, is the role they play in making alignment happen. All Change Agents are responsible to at least three people: their boss, the Target(s), and the Sustaining Sponsor.

What many miss is their responsibility to the Sustaining Sponsor. *They fail at connecting to the boss over the people where the change is taking place.* The Change Agent responsibilities chart shows the key relationships that exist here. The Change Agent must connect and stay in touch with the Targets, and they must always keep the Sustaining Sponsor informed. Who is your target? Who is their boss? Have you talked to the boss about what you are doing? Has your boss paved the way? Does the Sustaining Sponsor know how much of the Target's time you will need to complete the work? Have you talked about what they are learning and how to monitor? All these items are the Change Agent's responsibility.

They are also responsible to keep the system in alignment by highlighting moments when their boss and the Sustaining Sponsor of the work are out of sync. To do this, of course, they must stay in touch with both.

Change Agents can also help the work be more effective by talking to the Sustaining Sponsor and asking them to pave the way for effective change. By this, I mean help them think through what to say to get the employee (target) in line with the change or task. *Many managers need help in this arena and all Change Agents know how they wish the targets were working with them.* If, as a Change Agent, you think this through, you will find yourself in situation after situation where the targets are ready to do the work, rather than resistant or surprised that you are even there.

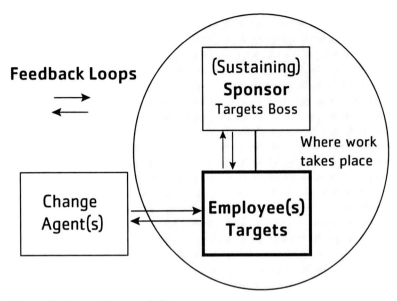

Figure 7 Target Responsibilities

Explanation of Figure 7

From your Sponsor (your boss): Get clarity of goals, enough time to complete the task, and boundaries. Since you have unique expertise doing the work, highlight any issues, gaps, or steps that you think will not work. Stay updated on progress. Work priorities on an as-needed basis. Ask for appropriate decision clarity to help the work happen as rapidly as possibly (if applicable).

From the Change Agent(s): Get help to do the work. Raise all issues that could impact the work. Stay in dialogue if there is any confusion about instructions, new methods, or processes they are teaching. Point out gaps in priorities between the expectations of the Sponsor and the items the Change Agent is trying to get accomplished. Say no and facilitate talks with Sponsor and Change Agent if misalignment is happening and is not being resolved.

Targets have a unique position in all organizations, as they are responsible to work with the Change Agent on the day-to-day tasks or change, and they must pay attention to their primary responsibility given to them by their boss (Sponsor).

Make no mistake here. Almost all Targets will drop what any Change Agent wants in order to please the person who is doing their performance evaluation, who just happens to be their boss. The Target also has a responsibility that most are unaware of or not used to providing, however. *They must raise all issues keeping them from reaching the bottom-line goals.*

The difficulty with this task in most environments is underplayed. Most Targets know what the problems are and which solutions handed down by management won't work. Few work in an organization that actually nurtures or seeks out that information. Rather, employees go to work and get instructions through a meeting structure that discourages dialogue and feedback. Some workplaces go as far as viewing asking questions or raising issues as resistance or making trouble.

Nonetheless, the job of the Target is to raise issues that could keep the organization from reaching its goals and to point out areas or moments when the Change Agent and Sustaining Sponsor are out of alignment. By this, I mean that the boss says, "I want this done right now as a high priority." Along comes the Change Agent who then wants a different priority. (Remember, it is just another co-worker trying to get a task done that involves the Target!) At this point the Target must help align the system by working the misalignment with the Change Agent and, if need be, get the two of them together to gain clarity of priorities.

It's a difficult task, indeed, as Targets are rarely invited to the table when problems are being solved. Very often, problems are solved by a combination of managers and technical experts without the added knowledge of the people who work in the area where there is a problem. Ironically, Targets almost always know when things are not working faster than anybody else in an organization; yet, too often, they are ignored. Ignore your targets and expect lackluster results from their area. Treat them as a customer and, paradoxically, you will gain real, lasting results. Target expertise is the missing ingredient to many problems facing organizations. (See Chapter 9 on p. 139.) Their unique knowledge is rarely listened to, usually under-utilized and, at worst, considered resistance.

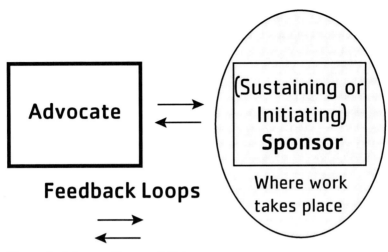

Figure 8 Advocate Responsibilities

Explanation of Figure 8

From the right Sponsor: Learn who the appropriate Sponsor is in the area where you want something different to happen. Find out how that Sponsor likes to hear information. Ask for time to present your data and the preferred format in which that Sponsor wants to receive it. If the Sponsor says yes to your idea, help coach them on how to effectively sponsor the change, based on the principles of this chapter. If they say yes, you are now in the role of a Change Agent, so you must adjust to helping facilitate the change. If the Sponsor says maybe, follow up a few more times. If the Sponsor says no, find a way to let go, or you risk personal and professional retribution. Retribution could be that you are perceived as pushy and hard to work with, or any other variation based on the workplace culture.

Advocates have a unique responsibility in an organization. *Their goal is to be heard.* Each of us has been an Advocate. Whenever you want something different, you are, by definition, an Advocate.

Your job is to find the right Sponsor. This can be easy or it can be very difficult. I have talked with many in organizations who are fed up with something fundamental that they want changed and are completely frustrated with the lack of progress. The dilemma is if they maintain that kind of frustration and intensity, they will surely become a problem to the leadership and perhaps to others.

To those advocating minor change: be sure when you articulate your proposal to your boss that you clearly describe what it is, the benefits, and any potential pitfalls. Since most in the role of Advocate are excited about their ideas, it is easy to oversell. Beware of that trap. The objective is to help your Sponsor understand and let the idea sell itself through clarity and dialogue.

To those trying to change how fundamental things are accomplished, your task is greater. You must learn who the right person to sponsor the change is within your organization. Then you must learn how that person wants to receive information as well as get permission to share your idea. They may like loads of data or they may want just a few bullets as to how it will change the organization. Not knowing this could kill your one chance for success. Once you learn how they want data, present the idea as descriptively and factually as possible.

Be honest without overselling. State likely benefits as well as potential pitfalls. After you have presented, if you get an immediate *yes* then you can start working with the Sponsor on how to go forward. If you get a *maybe* then follow up a few more times, but if you get a *no*, then you have the hardest task. All Advocates must learn how to let go of their beliefs in order for them to maintain solidarity in their current situation. New leaders may later emerge who want to implement your idea, but pushing hard once you have gotten a "no" may do irreparable damage to you in the organization.

Advocacy is tricky business because it involves sharing and letting others decide. If you alone made this decision, it would be simple. The reality, however, is that you are an Advocate rather than a Sponsor. Live within your role and you can have greater influence. Over-function by pushing too hard and you will suffer the consequences.

The Adventure Gets Real

Late the same week, the CEO calls a meeting with his lead team . . .

"OK, let's start. I need to talk to you because we are embarking on a mission-critical project and I am realizing that I have not done the work of talking to you yet. My bad, but here we are."

"What, a mission-critical project?"

"Yes, that is right. Ed and I have hired Jane Rogers. She is a highly qualified product manager and is going to take on the SMART project as the project manager. She will report to Ed. I know you all understand this, but a project this large will begin to put a real strain on our resources."

"What do you mean?" one lead team member responded. "I am already overloaded!"

Joe, looking a little surprised asked, "Overloaded?, how?"

"Joe, I have 30 other projects in my department. I can't possibly do another," said someone else.

"What?" Joe replied, his surprise turning to shock. "30 other projects?"

"Yeah. Me, to. All are critical and need to be done ASAP!" said yet another.

"Really? According to who?" asked Joe.

When Joe asked this, a long pause settled over the room, and the managers all started looking around; each looked puzzled by the statement. "Joe," the director of marketing said, "It's according to YOU!"

"Me? What?" (See p. 34.)

"Yes, just last week you added two more in my department."

"What?"

"Yes!" Frank spoke up. "That is my case as well?"

"Just what are these projects that I added?" At that point the discussion turned from shock and surprise to one of discovery. Joe learned of project after project that he had never intended to assign as well as many that he knew were mission-critical. What he then learned was that his ideas were taken as directives, especially if he was frustrated. When he found things not working, he tended to start spewing ideas and rarely, if ever, identified them as just thoughts. *Because he is the CEO, employees were taking what he said and running with it, whether he wanted them to or not.*

Suddenly Joe had an idea. "OK, I can see I have really been all over the map. This is what I need you all to do. Make a list of all the projects you have in your departments. Write the description as best you can, paying careful attention to the completion date and resource needs—especially if those resources are outside of your department. Let's reconvene tomorrow to better understand the mess we are in. In the meantime, I will talk with the board, the CFO, and Marketing and get really clear on our direction. Tomorrow we will meet and gain clarity about direction, then go over the projects."

"Here are two more things, *I want you to tell your people that if I start giving suggestions, they are not to move on them unless you clear it.* Of course, I will still walk around and see how things are going, but I have created a new goal for myself to really be engaged with you and make decisions based on conversations and facts. No more spouting off directives: clearly that has not worked. Folks, I need your help here to accomplish this. Please speak up if you think I am violating my own rules. I won't always like it, but I have to do this or we shall suffer."

"Seriously, Joe, you expect my employees to tell you no?"

"Well, yes, but at least I want them to be able to clear it with you. I know I have not been the greatest at listening to people, but I also know that if I do not try to change myself, I cannot expect others to. So, yes, please ask them to say no to me if they think I am directing them to do a special project."

"Joe, it will never work!" said Frank.

"Frank, it has got to. Our employees need to know we are in a tough situation and we must all be open to change, real change."

Ed and Jane arrived at Tim's office. Joe went separately.

Ed started, "Hi, Tim, not sure when Joe will be here, lots going on at work. I have read Chapter 3 that you gave us when we left as supplemental reading. I think I am clear."

"Great!" said Tim. "So what are you understanding?"

"Well, we have to create a bunch of roles for this project and they have to perform certain actions. Not really sure if it will work but I am clear about what you are saying. Clearly I am initiating this Project so I am the sponsor and since Jane is in such a critical role I may as well make her a—what did you call it—Sustaining sponsor."

Tim looked calm again, like he was sitting on something, but instead of speaking to Ed, he talked to Jane and said, "So how did you make sense of the chapter?"

"Well," Jane said, "I agree with much of what Ed says, but it seems to me that the role of Change Agent fits me better, even though I am fearful of my power and influence in such a role. Perhaps I should just go with the role of Sponsor."

At that moment, Joe rushed through the door, "Sorry I am late! Wow, what a week I am having!"

Ed chimed in, "No problem. We were just talking about Chapter 3 with Tim."

"Oh," Joe said. "Boy, that is a confusing chapter. Why would we create those new roles anyway?"

Jane spoke, "You have had a bad week?"

"No, not really bad, but revealing. I met with my lead team and found out that my actions are creating havoc all over the place. Did you know we have over 150 projects running simultaneously? They all are to be done ASAP, and they all need about 15 of the same resources."

"Wow," Tim said, "that is a lot, but unfortunately common. Most try to do too much. Despite the fact that resource constraints have only gotten tighter over the last few decades, the trends are clear. Do more with less, and find new ways to optimize."

"So what did you do?" asked Jane.

"Well, first I gave instructions for how to handle me; I know it won't solve it but it's a start. Then each department listed their projects and named the resources needed to complete them. I also had them state the projected end dates. Later, we reconvened in the large meeting room where we projected the list on the screen so it could be seen by all. From there, I explained the current state of the business and why we are embarking on the SMART project. That one was an eye-opener. It's like nobody really knew. In fact, most thought that we were in better shape than we actually are, while the reality is the competitors are breathing down our necks.

We were then able to stop about half of the projects. On 20 or so I have people looking at the impact on the business over time, but most were no-brainers once the group had clarity."

"Wow, Joe, I am impressed. You are on the path of managing from the middle. Nice job."

Joe went on, "So, what are we going to do about these new roles we have to create?"

Tim, finally responding to their understanding of the chapter said, "Well, not exactly what I hoped you would understand from the chapter. In fact, I must inform you, that you all seemed to miss a central point."

Ed speaks up, "What? Come on, Tim. It's pretty basic stuff!"

"Well, Ed," Tim continued, "that is a common thought, but an inaccurate one. Most really struggle to get this but when they do, real transformation can occur."

Jane now enters, "So, what *is* the point?"

Tim responded, "The point is that **these are not roles to create. They already exist** at all moments in every situation. The trick is to understand the current systemic dynamics in each unique situation and operate within them to ensure success or your system will likely get out of |balance. Just like the current state of the SMART project. Jane, you will not stand a chance unless you can help get Joe and Ed to leverage the right people in your business."

"Well, OK," Ed spoke up. "So, if that's true, what role am I in?"

"Your Jane's boss so you're her Sponsor, that makes you a Sustaining Sponsor; however, you are also an Advocate and a Change Agent. You must spread the word throughout the organization, but unlike Joe, you only hold one person accountable through legitimate authority. In other words, you do Jane's performance review and set her goals and objectives. That is unique power, yet not the only power."

"Jane, since you have no direct reports, you are a Change Agent. And Joe, you're the CEO, the single point above all who are part of this change; therefore, you are the Initiating Sponsor."

"Initiating? I did not initiate half of the projects that we talked about with my lead team today!"

"Yes, Joe, but if two departments are trying to get something done and they both report to you, then you are the Initiating Sponsor. It is definitional."

Jane looked bummed. Noticing this Tim asked, "What is it, Jane?"

"Well, it's just that if I understand the role of the Change Agent, it means I have no authority. How can I get things done?"

Ed chimes in, "Yeah, I am head of technology. How am I supposed to influence when the people who have to change are all over the business?"

Joe also joined in, "Right, and I am the CEO, yet you want me to focus just on my direct reports! Come on, Tim. Are we all off here?"

"Well, actually yes, and no. I do want you to pay much more attention to the realities of authority in your business and to believe that if you do not, you will never reach your goals. However, you all have a tremendous amount of power and influence in this organization. If you learn about it, learn to leverage it, and do not overdo some types of it, then you will influence the business in positive ways that you could not conceive of. Joe, you have the most leverage, obviously, because of your position, yet you were not fully leaning into that leverage in a positive way until this week. That meeting you just had, with your directs to gain clarity of initiatives, was an amazing start."

Tim continued, "You were all highly successful prior to meeting me. It is not like I want you to change that; I only want you to focus your awareness in certain situations, so that you can leverage yourselves appropriately and ensure that the business, as a whole, gets healthier and healthier."

"Let me get really clear on some specifics of what I am trying to say." From there, Tim began delineating the types of power that exist in organizations and perhaps, most importantly, how to use power in a positive way. He illustrated how Ed, Joe, and Jane could begin utilizing their unique life learnings and positions in the business to greater influence people. Afterwards Tim suggested another supplemental chapter to read between meetings.

◊◊◊

Read Chapter Four

CHAPTER 4

Power

"I'm only a Change Agent. I have no power!"

—countless employees

The most basic way to think of power in organizations is in terms of legitimate power. Either I am or I am not the boss. However, there are many other types of power at play in every organization that contribute to its failure or success. Many discount their potential to positively impact the organization, out of a lack of clarity and understanding of their power. Many are also confused about how to use their power in a generative versus de-generative way.

I want you to be clear about the many forms of power that exist and learn how to use them in a generative way in order to help your organization to be as successful as possible. To further explore power, I will begin with the definition of generative power and then explore many of the different types of power.

Generative Power

At the core of this book resides a critical ingredient in organization success: the intersection between authority, power, and love. However, since the words *power* and *love* are so confused in our culture, I am appreciative of Adam Kahane for the clarity I seek to convey. Kahane, in his recent book *Power and Love* synthesizes a view of power and love from some of the great minds of our time such as Martin Luther King Jr and Paul Tillich. When the people in your organization learn how to leverage their power and love, as defined below and in the ways outlined throughout this book, then you will reach record results.

Tillich defined *power* as "the drive of everything to realize itself, with increasing intensity and extensity." So, power in this sense is the drive to achieve one's purpose, to get one's job done, to grow. He defines *love* as "the drive towards the unity of the separated." So, love in this sense is the drive to reconnect and make whole that which has become or appears fragmented. These two ways of looking at power and love, rather than the more common ideas of oppression and romantic love, are at the core of his book *Power and Love* and reflect the type of power and love that, if nurtured and utilized, helps organizations thrive.

In the words of Martin Luther King, drawing on his doctoral studies of Tillich's work:

> "Power properly understood is nothing but the ability to achieve purpose. It is the strength required to bring about social, political, and economic change . . . And one of the great problems of history is that the concepts of love and power have usually been contrasted as opposites—polar opposites—so that love is identified with the resignation of power, and power with the denial of love. Now we've got to get this thing right. What (we need to realize is) that power without love is reckless and abusive and love without power is sentimental and anemic.
>
> . . . It is precisely this collision of immoral power with powerless morality which constitutes the major crisis of our time."

—Martin Luther King Jr.,
"Where Do We Go From Here?"

The opposite of power and love is not hate but indifference. From here, Kahane postulates two types of power: *generative* and *de-generative*. Examples of *generative power* in organizations are aligning the system to its real challenges, holding people accountable, ensuring conflicts get resolved so that work gets accomplished on-time and with quality between people and departments, and various forms of praise and acknowledgment to employees for hard work and accomplishments. *De-generative power* can be seen as avoidance of issues, allowing employees to do whatever they want, forced separation of people or departments that must work together as a way of "coping," punishing people for speaking out or raising difficult work issues, and spreading negative rumors. All employees, especially those in positions of authority, must find ways to use their power in generative ways and minimize or eliminate their use of de-generative power.

Organizations complicate these two types of power because all humans have at least some issues with authority figures leftover from childhood. *The more issues with authority one has, the easier it is to see authority, by the very fact that it exists, as mostly de-generative.* Therefore, those highly impacted by this struggle are more likely to have only known or been able to see de-generative power. They may miss the promise, potential, and importance of nurturing generative power. A mature adult development stage is to recognize that bosses (and all of us) possess both. Yet, some need appropriate guidance, education, and opportunities to nurture and grow their use of generative power. Workplaces seduced by de-generative power are more apt to think consensus is best, raising issues is tattling, controlling through indirect means is appropriate, lacking clarity about decisions is common and, worse, operating like this should be the norm.

This book is about nurturing generative power in your organization in order to help *all* employees get on the same page. Do this and you will successfully navigate the complexities of your business.

Types of Power

This section offers clarity about how to leverage the most common types of power through your current position to most effectively impact the organization. Please note: each type of power can be used in a generative or de-generative way. It is my hope that you gain clarity about the power that you are utilizing and learn how to use it generatively in order to help your organization thrive. The four classic types of power are legitimate, interpersonal, expertise, and referent.

Legitimate Authority—This is the authority granted to bosses to whom at least one employee reports, and who does the employee's(s') performance review. If you are a boss, yet do not have the authority to both hire and fire your employees, then you do not have legitimate authority, even if you are a shift leader or supervisor. In that case, you must study how to be a good Change Agent, because that is the reality of authority with which you are operating.

Interpersonal—Often referred to as trust, it goes far deeper, partially because trust is built with effective interpersonal communication skills. The ability to manage tense moments, the ability to tune into people who are having problems, and the ability to do all of this in a way that honors both you and others is a rare talent. Interpersonal power can been seen in all organizations as the person who gets high respect, people like interacting with, and have high, yes, trust. Interpersonal power is a learned skill that can be built by increasing one's ability to manage tense moments with grace. In other words, by increasing one's Emotional Intelligence (EQ).

Expertise—Expertise power comes from one's experiences, skills, or knowledge. It is gained over time through working in a particular area or by training in a topic, process, machine, etc. It is often referred to as knowledge or skill power. It is about having a deeper understanding of an area so that people see you as an "expert" in it. External consultants are experts who leverage their expertise power.

Referent—Referent authority is how other people talk about you. This power is gained by being thought well of by people whom others trust. If the employees who work on the floor of any plant are in conflict with management, who would you want with you while walking through the floor? I hope you're a fast learner. Yes, of course, it would be a trusted person on the floor. Referent power is about whom you know and their standing in the group with whom you are presently working.

The reason all of the above matters is that many, if not most, in organizations are confused about their actual power. Due to this confusion they either over- or underplay their role. Machine specialists think that because they have technical expertise, the managers or workers have to do what they say. Yet, they may know neither how to utilize interpersonal power nor how to leverage legitimate power. (See p. 104 of Chapter 6.)

Change Agents may believe, due to their lack of legitimate authority in the system, that they have no power in any situation. Yet, at the very least, they bring expertise power. They also can learn how to increase their interpersonal power and how to leverage the legitimate authority that exists in all scenarios. Leveraging legitimate authority builds system alignment to the change and increases the chance of its success.

Managers often do not know how to leverage either their legitimate authority or interpersonal power to improve the working relationships outside of their span of control. They may get stuck in one or the other. Some managers want to be liked so much (an "over-doing" of interpersonal power) that they forget how to use their legitimate authority.

Employees are often too fast or too slow in utilizing their interpersonal or referent power, either creating tension or missing easy opportunities to increase system alignment. Having clear understanding of these concepts eliminates confusion and increases productivity.

Yet, there is more. Gain clarity on these additional types of power so you can increase your effectiveness.

Personal Authority—This is an EQ-related power. Each of us possesses the capability to say or do whatever we need to, whenever we need to, even if the situation is extremely tense. Personal authority is the capability to choose, and be however you need to be, no matter what you are feeling. Take an appropriate stand, say what you think or want, differ in appropriate ways to all levels of employees and, above all, choose your behavior rather than use the learned reactive responses developed throughout your life. The capability to say no, to hold people accountable, to let go of decisions, to take more ownership, etc. are all components of personal authority.

It is also the power that you need to hold your employees accountable: No personal authority and your employees will know they do not really have to listen to you. Since personal authority is about EQ, it is by definition learned and, therefore, it can be increased throughout your lifetime. It is difficult to increase, however. The best path I know of is through hard work and experiential education. *Sorry, you can't just read a book or go to a lecture.* To increase EQ you must try on behaviors, feel the experience, reflect on the experience, and begin to work through the emotional reactivity that reduces the flexibility of your current behavioral patterns. The use of personal authority is not to be confused with being inappropriate. It is about clearly articulating your wants, holding people accountable, having the freedom to act, and being able to function, no matter the situation, in balanced, appropriate ways.

The Power of the Purse—This power is perhaps the most widely used power in organizations and, unfortunatly, often used de-generatively. Money is a major resource that stops or starts activities. The power of the purse is literally the power to spend. Think "spending authority." Is there a budget you are working within? If so, can you decide how to spend on resources, trainings, supplies, or do you have to get approval? At what level?

Do you decide if a machine, consultant, training, supply, or raw material is a worthwhile expenditure for your department or position, or do you have to get sign-off approval on most things? Does your boss tell you to work within your budget and spend however you need to in order to get business results? Or, does your boss require his approval before you can spend, and then often say "No," even if you think this expenditure is necessary to reach your business goals? The power of the purse is a major power within all organizations.

Legal—This type of expertise is used in many ways, such as defending against injustice or unwarranted lawsuits. It is also used to inform employees about behaviors that may put the organization at risk of a lawsuit. Many organizations have lawyers embedded, intended to protect the business and, of course, many do a stellar job.

The downside comes when the embedded lawyer is risk-averse and their advice is followed too rigidly. In such a culture, policies start to manage people and conflict is pushed under the table. If you say the wrong words while venting during a conflict, the legal fear trumps the ability to continue the conversation and find resolution.

Thus, restrictive boundaries may get set that do not allow people to talk directly when in conflict or managers to give straightforward feedback when an employee is under-performing. Therefore, healthy resolution is not allowed between the conflicted parties and learning, for each individual and the overall system, gets stifled.

Healthy conflict resolution includes a structure to talk things through directly, a plan to address a similar situation in the future, and a way to identify and resolve the systemic issues contributing to the situation. If employees are not allowed to talk to each other, the emotional reactivity in the culture will grow as the real issues are not solved and, rather, are pushed under the table.

Since restricting conversations is the norm in such situations, there is a greater chance of "witch hunts" where investigations happen by HR and, at the advice of a restrictive lawyer, decide who is right or wrong, and what the punishment is.

Contrast that with a culture which assumes most conflicts come from misunderstandings. In these cultures, parties to the conflict are provided with the opportunity to explore their reactions and learn from each other. The learning goes beyond reactive judgments to the specific behaviors which occurred and, once grounded and ready to listen, to finding out the true intent of the other. At that point, problem-solving and healing may occur with greater ease.

Ownership—If I own something then I can also use it in any way I like. If I own a chair I can set fire to it, which I couldn't do if I had borrowed it from you. If I own money, I can spend it anyway I choose. Ownership power is part and parcel of sole proprietor or family-owned businesses. The dynamics here are much different than with a corporate-run business. Owners normally have a much harder time trying to let go of decision making than corporate-run businesses do. Whatever family dysfunction or health exists will echo throughout the business.

Positional—The higher in an organization you go, whether or not you have direct reports, the more positional power you obtain. Most employees treat members of the lead team differently than managers at lower levels.

Positional power is also the power given by roles, such as quality auditors on the floor, technical specialists, human resources, and others. Where you occupy a recognized position, then I will obey the rules regarding that position (rather than obeying you, per se). Formal positions include managers, policemen, and so on. These may well have formal authority vested in them by the company or the country.

Informal—This power is cumulative and comes from years of experience, common sense, and effective interpersonal power. All workplaces have informal leaders who are important in situations where employees are skeptical about a direction or proposal. Often, these are informal leaders who can persuade undecided people to resist or conform.

Access—When you are given the power to gain or deny access, you have been granted access power. Company receptionists, roles responsible for areas such as training or safety, are often gatekeepers within the organization. Personal assistants control access to the managers they serve. Librarians control access to the materials in the library within which they work.

Along with this particular power comes the customer service experience of *first impressions*. Often the access person, or voice in recent years, is the first experience customers have within your organization. Over the last 30 years, ironically, most organizations have opted to let go of having a human perform this task and instead rely on automated phone systems. Since access power is about first impressions, there is a huge industry built up on how to improve your access power. Access power is part of your customer's experience. If you miss this, you may be adding undue tension and stress to your customers' interactions.

Coercive—Coercive power is conveyed by increasing the fear of losing one's job, being demoted, receiving a poor performance review, having prime projects taken away, etc. This power is accrued by threatening others. For example, the VP of Sales who threatens sales folks to either meet their goals or get replaced is an example of coercive power. Beware: this is a "dark power": its misuse can significantly damage workplace morale. Low morale is directly correlated with poor business performance. Coercive power is tempting because it is easy to use. In contrast, it is much harder to take the time with your employees to get clear on direction, what the business needs are and why, then involve them to get there. The use of a little coercive power is probably OK, but beware of overusing it.

Reward—Reward power is conveyed through rewarding individuals for compliance with one's wishes. This may be done through given bonuses, raises, a promotion, extra time off work, etc. For example, the supervisor who provides employees comp time when they meet an objective she had set for a project. Reward power is often misused in organizations, as many confuse motivation with financial reward.

The one type of reward that all psychologists agree works is positive reinforcement. However, it is only effective if the reinforcement is timely, genuine, and behaviorally specific. Saying "Good job" may be nice, but it is not an example of effective positive reinforcement. Say it all the time and you will begin to lose trust. Some of the most hated managers got into huge conflicts from misunderstanding how to use reward power. Most were genuinely trying to be nice, yet were never specific in their praise. All were totally confused as to how others could be upset with them, since they had intended to convey positive reinforcement.

The list in this chapter surely omits other types of power that exist. My intention here is to be clear about a dynamic critical within most, if not all, organizations. If you clarify and align the employees in positions that have legitimate authority in your system and point them towards a more generative use of power, then you will create a culture that will achieve record results and have high morale. Ignore this and the other types of power will run your organization more likely in de-generative ways, sometimes, literally into the ground. Several types of power are evident at any given time in all organizations. By increasing your awareness and understanding of them while focusing on their generative use, you can increase your organization's effectiveness.

Help Me Understand

A half hour later, Jane, Ed, and Joe all seemed visibly calmer. The room was filled with afternoon light and the talk about power and influence cleared up many misconceptions.

Jane spoke up. "OK, now I get it, I think I was over-reacting earlier. I have a ton of ability and know that. I just thought you said I had no way to influence or help people be accountable."

Joe spoke, "It's actually quite the opposite. What you know must be shared and leveraged or the business will not succeed! You are a gold mine for this group; it may be that they just don't know it yet. Yet what I am getting here, and hopefully Jane and you, Ed, are also seeing it, is that by holding people accountable, we help ensure real sponsorship is in place, and the right people, the Sponsors, are doing their job."

"Wow," said Ed.

"But," Joe continued, "what I am learning about myself is that I relied too much on coercion and controlling through top-down cost controls. I gave threats, made rules that forced how people spent money, and did not allow them to think independently."

Tim spoke up, "That is a great realization, Joe. Many CEOs, corporate headquarters, and top-level managers miss that. They instead overuse control through purse strings. *Real power lies in being clear, setting boundaries, increasing interpersonal abilities, sharing problems, and engaging the hearts and minds of your employees to work with you to solve your problems.* I have seen too many workplaces and managers who impose solutions and restrictions from above rather than gain clarity of purpose and then give appropriate support and guidance to solve things. The statistics are clear: engage with clarity and boundaries and you will not only increase morale but achieve better results. If you go top-down and impose solutions while tightly restricting money so people cannot choose or think for themselves, then you will start a long slow spiral."

Joe commented, "Wow! That is a great point and so simple. Yet, why do I think it won't be that easy? I can see we have been on that spiral. It is time to stop the cycle."

"Nice, Joe! And I think the reality is that *simple does not mean easy* but with hard work it will pay off."

Joe continued, "But, Tim, going back to what I've learned, I have also not utilized my ability to talk to people and leverage my *generative power* capabilites. I am great with the board, but I forget about it when I talk to people under me. I can now see that has got to change."

Ed also spoke up, "Yes and I have relied too much on my technology knowledge to win arguments, I forget to listen and understand at times. I have got to make a note to change that."

At that point Jane spoke up, "Ed, I also have noticed that, and if it works for you, I will help hold your feet to the fire when I see it happening. Like last week when we were talking to the programmers; I still don't think we understood their issue, yet you kept going."

Ed, looked perplexed and a little embarrassed, but hung in and stated, "Wow, you are right, and that is sort of my typical MO. Thanks, Jane, your feedback and help is much appreciated."

Tim spoke up, "Jane, that is awesome, and thank you for your courage in saying that. Generative power is for all employees to leverage in whatever way they can; it is possible to get a critical mass of employees who know how to and willing to use generative power. (See *Cultural Change in Organizations,* Appendix B.) I imagine, Ed, that you both respected it, yet felt a little embarrassed. If you all pledge to help each other in tense moments, you can really make a difference to the organization as a whole."

"Great point, Tim," Joe said. "I for one would welcome the help!"

"Agreed," added Jane.

"Tim," Jane continued talking and redirected the conversation, "I gotta tell you that I think I sort of understand, what did you call it? Sponsor Agent Target Advocate? But I am still about as clear as mud on it. Can you help me understand by giving me some examples?

"Sure, Jane, I am glad you asked. Most people struggle with this theory. They even think I am pushing a program or new model. I am not. Rather this is a tool, *a tool to highlight what exists is all organizations everywhere.* Let me show you what I mean by charting a few basic scenarios. I will start as simple as possible, then I will give you some more complex situations. The principles are always the same, but they can get tricky, and most struggle to comprehend them."

"Excellent!"

"Yes!" A near simultaneous reply came from Ed and Joe. "Since I am also clear as mud!"

Tim then went to the board and started to chart out a basic scenario . . .

◊◊◊

Read Chapter Five

CHAPTER 5

SATA Workplace Examples

The Initial Analysis for Every Situation

SATA is not easy, but it is simple. Following up the definitions given in Chapter 3, we will analyze different business scenarios. My intention is to help you understand SATA by showing it in action.

Scenario number 1—Maintenance to the Floor

Shown below is a typical relationship between maintenance and the floor. In this scenario, maintenance mechanic 1 is trying to get work done with shift worker 1. The work takes place on the floor. The critical question is who sponsors the work? Choose your answer prior to looking at the chart on the next page.

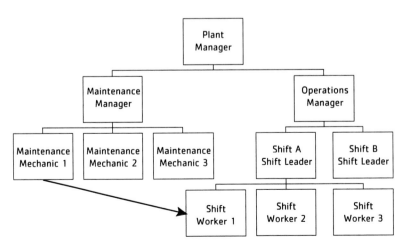

Figure 9 Scenario 1

Here is the answer -

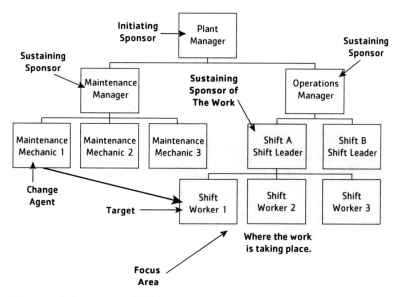

Figure 10 Scenario 1 SATA Map

In the chart above, I have shaded the focus area where the work takes place. *That is the key to understanding sponsorship.* ***The Sponsor of the work is always the Sustaining Sponsor above the Target(s) where the work must take place.*** This point is critical and often missed. Many think that because it is maintenance working on the machine, it is the maintenance manager, but they are incorrect. Obviously, the maintenance manager is critical here, but what is most critical is that they are aligned with the floor. If the maintenance mechanic goes to do the work and the floor employee is not ready, then the chance of tension is high. The shift leader sets the priorities for the floor employees (normally with coordination of the day's schedule), and the employees in turn organize their work based on those priorities.

Notice that no Advocate is listed? That is because advocacy can come from any role. It begins when an employee wants something different than what is happening today. It could come from the shift leader, maintenance employee, maintenance manager, floor employee, or anyone else who wants a change which they think will improve work.

Were you surprised that the Operations Manager is a Sustaining Sponsor? All employees who are between the Sponsor of the work and the

Initiating Sponsor are, by definition, Sustaining Sponsors. Therefore, the operations manager is a Sustaining Sponsor, albeit a key one, yet not the most critical for the work to happen smoothly. If the operations manager does not provide clear expectations to the shift leader, then work may suffer (in Chapter 11, I explain this further in a segment titled "The Black Hole of Sponsorship"). However, the most critical Sponsor of the work in this scenario is Shift Leader A. If they give Shift Worker 1 a different priority then the task will not get accomplished.

First Critical Distinction: Remember the word Sponsor is used to define two types of Sponsors: the Sustaining Sponsor and the Initiating Sponsor. *The Initiating Sponsor is the single person above all people involved, by definition.* Internal to one organization, there can only be one Initiating Sponsor per situation. All other Sponsors are Sustaining Sponsors, i.e., if the Sponsor above the people you are working with has a boss, then that person is a Sustaining Sponsor. *If fact, all bosses between the Target and the Initiating Sponsor are Sustaining Sponsors.*

Why does it matter? When Sponsors are misaligned, then they may unknowingly set conflicting priorities that hurt productivity. Understand this dynamic and you will see alignment problems faster, plus be able to help the right people talk to each other to clear them up. Once you do this, you will quickly help work get done or perhaps find out that it is you who are working on the wrong stuff. If you do not examine this when problems arise, your system will miss opportunities to self-correct.

Second Critical Distinction: Identifying the Sponsor and whether they are supporting the work are two different things. Many Sponsors do not even know about the work. In Chapter 3, I wrote: "By definition, the direct boss of whom you are trying to work with IS the Sponsor of that person. Whether they support what you are trying to do is another story." There is a huge difference between identifying the Sponsor and having that Sponsor being effective at "Sponsoring the work." *Helping the Sponsor become effective is the major task of the Change Agent.* Of course, if you find out the Sponsor does not want what you are trying to get accomplished, then you are in the role of the Advocate. Your next task is to gain system alignment for your particular change and/or learn how to let it go if you find out that the task, indeed, is not supported.

Scenario number 2—Implementing a Daily Floor Walk

Below represents a small manufacturing plant. In this scenario, the new plant manager wants to start a system of daily walk-throughs on the floor using a whiteboard to track issues. The daily walk-throughs must be attended by the manager and a few key personnel from maintenance, quality, the warehouse, scheduling, and engineering. It is to be led by the floor personnel.

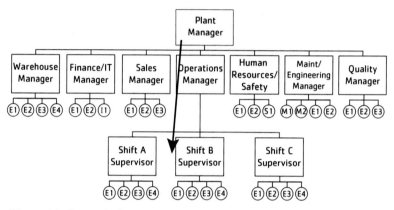

Figure 11 Scenario 2

The work is taking place on the floor, but it requires coordination of most of the system to do it well. So, who is the Sponsor of the work?

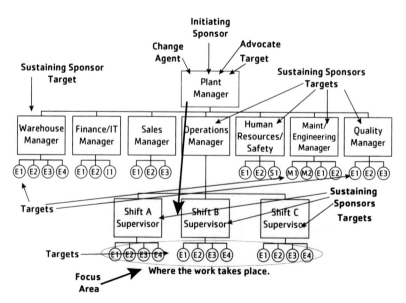

Figure 12 Scenario 2 SATA Map

Here, again the focus area is the floor. *So, by definition, the Sponsors of the work are the three shift supervisors.* The Targets are the floor employees. It is not that simple, however, since department managers are also Targets. Notice also that in this scenario the Plant Manager is initiating the change. Due to this, he is in multiple roles. *Most employees are in multiple SATA roles at all times, but only a Sponsor can be in all four. That is so since to be a Sponsor, you must have a direct report.* In this case, he is the Initiating Sponsor of the overall work, the Sponsor to his direct reports, the Change Agent, the Advocate, and even a Target to the extent that he participates in the walk-through.

It is rare to have the Plant Manager be the Change Agent (see "When the Change Comes From the Top" on p. 175) but, in this situation, he was the only one who knew how to execute the new process. In the future someone else who has this expertise, or someone he trains, can become the Change Agent. In the scenario above, he is the Change Agent, currently the only one with that capability.

That means he must spend a lot of time educating and setting up the process of the daily walk-throughs. From the separate departments, each worker who must participate is a Target. I have therefore identified, from each department, each Target who will take place in the walk-through. They too must be educated and learn how to contribute from their roles.

A major change like this will mean that Sustaining Sponsors need to do a lot of work to get alignment within the system. They must ask questions for clarity and communicate any confusion to the Initiating Sponsor. They must also make sure their employees know what is expected, plus provide them with education, support, and enough time for implementation.

The Initiating Sponsor's task is to set the stage, to provide clarity and appropriate structure, and to continually follow up until success is achieved. In this unique case, the Initiating Sponsor is the plant manager and is *also* the most knowledgeable about the change. Therefore, he is also in the role of Advocate and *must* spend ample time *educating* the work force as to the "*why* and *what*" of the desired change.

Are you surprised that I said Advocate? *Remember that **you can only Sponsor your direct reports,** so you must be aware of the role you play in each scenario.* The plant manager in this case must hold his direct reports accountable and they, in turn, hold theirs until the whole organization is aligned. Beyond alignment, with a major change, such as initiating a daily walk-through, consistent and calm education, and follow-through to allow for minor tweaks until it works right is critical.

The Sustaining Sponsors in this scenario must continually be updated by the Change Agent, and react quickly to ensure proper execution and support. Part of this could be to ensure that department heads resolve work issues they may be avoiding, or to break ties when necessary.

A Sponsor who says "Go do it," without any oversight or check in, is abdicating rather than sponsoring. If they really support it, then the Sponsor must learn a balanced way of driving it to ensure success.

They must be thinking about the whole system, not just the people involved in the new process. If unaware of these dimensions, the initiative will surely fail, but not for the reasons normally associated with it, such as blaming the failure on one person or on the method used to problem solve. When systems are out of alignment, people unintentionally do things that thwart success without even knowing it.

The purpose of a walk-through is to help issues and problems surface and get worked through faster. The workers themselves are encouraged to advocate and surface issues instead of allowing them to stay undercover. Many ideas for changes and problems will surface. Therefore, there must be a structure in place to capture ideas that will help the process continually improve.

Not all ideas will nor can be implemented, but all should be understood and considered in a way that encourages input. The system will need a way to determine a) whether too much or too little is being taken on and b) how to continually monitor the work load. Each scenario is different, not just in layout but in the real technical and interpersonal capabilities of the personnel. So, continuing to tweak the change until it is producing consistent results is critical. This takes time and patience but it has been done time and again. If your efforts fail, ask yourself if you really put in enough effort to build effective sponsorship and if you created appropriate structures to slowly ensure success.

Failure is rarely caused by a new practice; rather, it is most often a result of poor implementation.

Scenario number 3—Software Development Integrated Billing

The chart below represents a large health care billing company that has recently merged four divisions. Their primary billing software is now operational and they are in the process of creating a unique integrated billing system intended to separate them from the industry, thus giving them a leg up on the market. The new software is being developed by the Senior Director Integration Strategy.

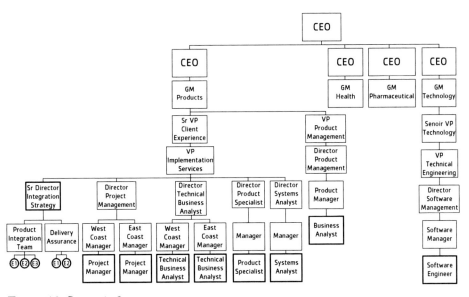

Figure 13 Scenario 3

The chart above identifies who is working to create the new software and shows the authority structure in the organization, up from each identified person.

Once again, the key question is: Who is the Sponsor of the work?

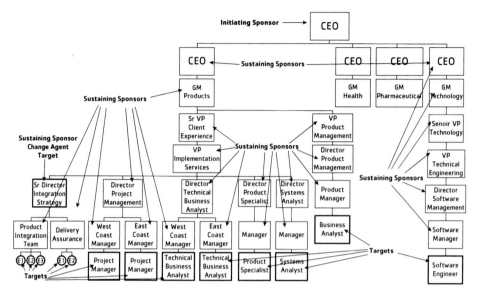

Figure 14 Scenario 3 SATA Map

In this case, sponsorship is complicated: A large business unit named "Products" creates the product specifications; however, the engineers developing the software operate under a completely separate business unit. Thus, the Initiating Sponsor is far removed from the actual work and may or may not be kept in the loop as to what is happening.

The Senior Director Integration Strategy is working with a large cross section of people to create the product specifications. He must dedicate time to inform the Sustaining Sponsors above those people about the ongoing time commitments needed to be successful or misalignment with other tasks could easily occur. The VP of Implementation has a large ongoing task to align the rest of the organization to the product. Notice, the only Change Agent I have identified on the chart is the Senior Director Integration Strategy. That is because he is the one who is clearly working with other groups to get things done. In reality, though, many will do the same in a project this large. Understanding what SATA role you play moment by moment and paying attention to the systemic dynamics are critical to get work done well and to maintain system health.

The GM of Products and the CEO over all the business units are at critical *systemic pinch points,* in conflicts over resources or alignment.

For example, if the Business Analyst two layers below the VP of Product Management is conflicted about which task is more important, the core software system or the one in development, then only the GM of Products can break the tie. The same is true for the Software Engineer five layers below the CEO of Technology. Only the CEO of all the business units is positioned in the system with the legitimate authority to break the tie. Not knowing either of those two facts could lead to competing resources and lack of alignment for weeks, months or, potentially, even years.

For this scenario to be successful, the goals have to be clear to all: *why* they are creating this product, *what* specifics they are working to create, and *when* it needs to be up and running in the marketplace to stay on top of the competition. Lack of clarity of goals here means the development process could continue for years. Implementing with clarity of goals, outlined in Chapter 2, will provide both clarity of alignment throughout through the system and enable work completion more easily.

On a project like this, it is key to make sure that all socio-technical components are in place and working effectively (see the checklist on p. 30).

Employees can be in multiple SATA roles!

Both of the last two scenarios have people such as the Initiating Sponsors in multiple roles. That is so because the roles are definitional. You can have as many as four SATA roles and a few as one. Everyone is in at least one role. If you have no employees reporting to you, the maximum you can be in is three roles (Change Agent, Advocate, and Target).

Online at Business Expert Press, I have several additional SATA workplace examples including implementing lean, expanding a program at a non-profit, leveraged buying in a corporation, and fundraising at a church.

Our Situation Is Unique

Later still, during the same session . . .

Jane spoke first. "Wow, OK, I think I am beginning to get it but what you gave me were standard situations; our situation is unique. We are different and, I might add, difficult. We are home-grown and have a unique platform, structure, and population."

"Yes," Joe chimed in. "None of what you just charted relates to us."

Suddenly you could feel the tension in the room.

"Crap, is this really what we need?" Ed blurted. "Can't we just tell people what to do and get it over with?"

"Hmmm. Well, that certainly is one strategy?" Tim replied.

"Um, Ed," Joe spoke up, "need I remind you that your strategy IS what we have been trying to do for quite some time. I think you know the results. Lets just say, NOT GOOD!"

"Yes, OK, but this seems hard, and complicated."

"That is true, Ed. It is hard and complicated. Or let me put it another way, it's as complicated as it is. *Whatever the reality is in your organization, it simply is. You might complain about it, but that does not shape or change it. It is only by being fully open to what is there that you can work with it to get the results you are looking for.* And I have never claimed that it is easy. Setting top-down controlling policy is quick, perhaps not easy, but certainly most of those types of policies have predictable results. What you are looking for is a new type of engagement in your organization in order to succeed in a difficult project that holds the key to your success. This will take hard work and persistence. The question you all need to ask is: are you up for being firm, committed, and persistent while you go through this process?"

"Look, Tim," Joe said, "I know what we have done has not worked. I don't fully get what you are saying yet, but I get enough to know that it is more in the right direction. I say we continue on. What next? Oh, and, Ed, I need you here. I am hoping you will come with me. We are obviously not aligned yet in our workplace; I think Tim here is showing us a path forward. *I am not asking for an easy path: I have tried too many of those in the past. I want an honest path, one that is grounded in reality and what is really happening inside our business."*

"It's OK, Joe," said Ed. "I guess I am just impatient. Let's continue."

"Whew!" Suddenly Jane let out a huge sigh of relief. "Wow, I was holding my breath there and was not even aware of it. I guess I had great fear about stopping and just trying to combat the organization without any more insights. I have learned some nice things here. Thank you, Joe and Ed, for agreeing to continue. Now, Tim, I asked you about our situation. How can we figure out our unique puzzle?"

"Nice, Jane. That is the next place to go. I have a repeatable process for this that can be used for any scenario. Are you all ready to get cooking?"

"OK, first off, let's write the timeline on the board. By when does this need to be completed?"

"Well, we are starting it and should work hard." Joe stated.

Tim broke in quickly, "Wait, Joe. I thought you said that you will lose market share unless you not only complete this, but also, the software that you create is high quality?"

Joe looked startled, "Well, yes, but I rarely actually give completion dates, I mean, that is so demoralizing."

"Hmmm. Joe, I think you have it backwards," said Tim. "Not being successful nor getting out in front is demoralizing. Absolute clarity with consequences known for the business is critical, or people have a hard time understanding your intensity and driving behavior. To get people on board, you have to be honest and real."

"Wow!" Joe replied. "I have always thought that my job was to protect my employees and not let them feel too much stress."

"Most research points to the opposite," said Tim. "Employees want honesty and real challenges. They want the truth. Once they know that, then they can get behind just about anything. If you come across as transparent and open, they usually respond in kind."

"OK, truth," answered Joe. "By next August, we have to finish this and get it to market. If not, we are in serious trouble."

"OK, good," Tim transitioned. "Now tell me all the players who have tasks on the project or who will have to do something differently as a result."

"The players?" Jane replied. "To do that we might as well put up the whole chart! Gosh, this is so big. Isn't there an easier way?"

"Well," Tim said, "of course. Why don't you just talk about an area that you predict will be a problem and we can apply the theory there?"

"What?" Joe said. "You want us to point the finger at people?"

"No, Joe," Tim continued, "this is about being honest and aligning the organization to the real needs of the business. If there is real conflict, you will only solve it by working through it. This analysis is intended not to get people in trouble, rather to create a path forward to success. It may reveal some hard work you must do interpersonally. I trust you are up to the task."

"Hmmm. You may be right. I think I have avoided difficult scenarios in the past. I get it that we have to move beyond that."

"OK, so you are ready?" Tim asked.

"YES!" Jane, Ed, and Joe simultaneously answered loudly, then started chuckling.

"Lets go!" Joe said.

"So, from my perspective, one clear troubled area is Marketing. It is odd, but the people in marketing don't seem to get this project. Yet, the carriers, our clients, love it. Any help there would be much appreciated."

"OK!" Tim said. "Lets start." From here, Tim went on to chart the unique workplace scenario Jane described and continued to educate them about the SATA realities within their business . . .

$$\Diamond\Diamond\Diamond$$

Read Chapter Six

CHAPTER 6

SATA Analysis

SATA is critical for scenarios such as planning huge initiatives or projects, but *perhaps its greatest contribution is as **an analysis tool** when work is stuck or in conflict.* To be clear, that means that if you are able to get work done there is no need to worry about SATA. If fact, if you are always successful completing your work, and you achieve world-class numbers, then you don't need to worry.

World-class companies earn that name for a reason; however, in reality most businesses have plenty of snags in their day-to-day work, large projects, or major initiatives. The excuses for these problems often miss the mark by focusing on individual thinking, such as employee resistance, rather than an honest assessment about the lack of understanding of how to build organization alignment. The former is personality theory; the latter is systems theory. I suggest *always* starting with systems theory, and in particular with SATA, as it relates to change roles, sponsorship, and alignment. The first step to create clarity in any situation is to conduct a SATA analysis by charting the employees impacted, identifying their SATA roles, and building a strategy to increase sponsorship.

What follows is a step-by-step process to do just that.

Basic Guidelines to Chart Any Scenario *(change or day-to-day work)*
1. Identify a current work scenario, which
   - involves a day-to-day task that gets stuck or struggles to be done effectively;
   - is a planned change, be it small to large; or
   - is a large project, involving people across many departments.

Stuck work could mean many things, such as a product change on the manufacturing floor that takes too long or a delay or improper decision about whether to scrap product which is being produced outside of specified standards, etc. Or it could be that you are trying to get help from another department and they are saying no!

2. Create a timeline with key events or milestones. Make the timeline from left to right on a flip chart or whiteboard with dates by week or by month, depending on the length of the item. I usually date by month with plenty of space in-between.

3. Draw your organization's chart of legitimate authority related to your work scenario. Include anyone with a task and those, if any, who will have to do things differently once implemented. Start the chart from all who have a task and all who will do things differently, then diagram the lines of legitimate authority up to a single boss above all on the list. If people on your chart work for a different organization, then you can have more than one Initiating Sponsor and, therefore, multiple charts. In Chapter 5, I have charted more examples if you wish further elucidation. The key is to include all who have a task or will use the item you are producing on your chart, as well as yourself.

Please note—Many create things in one department that will impact people in other areas of the organization. If that is the case with your scenario, *the people who are impacted in another area of the organization are by definition the Targets.* The most common error is to wait until implementation to engage the Targets. Thus, the knowledge of the Targets is missed and tension will rise.

4. Apply Sponsor/Agent/Target/Advocate to the situation.
   • Identify all SATA roles.
   • Identify key Sustaining Sponsors.
   • Identify your SATA role.

5. Circle all areas where there are problems.
   • Identify all areas that are potential or existing problems.
   • Identify key Systemic Pinch Points.
   • Assess your SATA roles (Appendix A: SATA Assessments).
   • Assess all SATA roles in circled areas.

6. Create change/communication plan based on your findings.
   - Use the analysis from steps 4 and 5 to formulate a strategy to improve your situation.
   - Chart all actions on timeline.
   - Circle back to appropriate Sponsor when things are stuck.
   - Work with the appropriate Sponsor(s) to leverage the change. *(Review p. 104 on leveraging change.)*

Since most struggle a bit to chart SATA, I have included an example following the steps I have outlined. I am skipping the timeline, as I think it is self-explanatory. This is the example that Jane brought Tim in our story. In this example, the Senior Product Manager is trying to create a new software system for their insurance carriers. The software involves most departments in the organization, yet Jane is worried that the Marketing department will be a challenge. Since her organization is so large, she just charted the area she is worried about and the organization up from her and down to the key players.

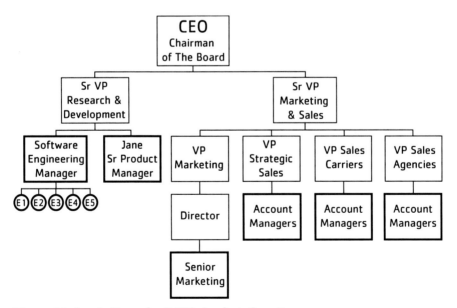

Figure 15 Jane's Example, SATA Analysis Step 3

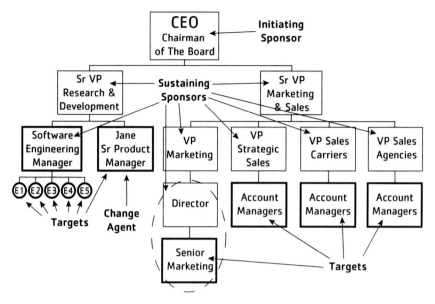

Figure 16 Jane's Example, SATA Analysis Step 4

The SATA chart gives you a visual of where, who, and what conversations need to happen in order to build alignment and increase the likelihood of success. In this example, the Change Agent (Jane) is concerned about the Senior Marketing person. Hence, the system may be out of alignment to the goals of the project. She must create a strategy to build sponsorship and get the workplace aligned, involving the key players. Further, the chart shows that the Sr VP of Research & Development, the Sr VP of Marketing and Sales, and the CEO are all in critical *systemic pinch points*. Finally, the Sr VP of Marketing and Sales has four departments to align to the goals of the project and the Sr VP of Research & Development must keep the Software Engineering Manager and the Product Manager on the same page. The CEO is the only one who has legitimate authority to break the tie between Research & Development and Marketing.

This data, combined with the assessments in Appendix A, will provide direction for Jane to move forward.

To further clarify, I have added a review of key principles of all SATA roles, now that you are at the point of charting and analyzing your system.

Review of Key Principles

Keys for Sponsors

You must remember to live by this key principle: You can only sponsor your direct reports, the people for whom you do their yearly performance review. There are rare occasions where it is not the case but, for the most part, it is. In the matrixed world we live in, there are many cases where people are assigned to you for projects or a short time period. The most functional way to ensure alignment during these moments is to have you do at least part of that person's performance review during that year. Make no mistake, all you Change Agents, Advocates, Targets, and other Sponsors (such as Initiating Sponsors trying to influence employees several layers under you) out there; *most employees really pay attention to whoever their direct boss is and who decides how well they are performing. (Most performance evaluations are tied to salary or wage increases in some way.)*

Beyond this, learn how to drive work through to results, to manage change, and to build organization alignment. Your job as a Sponsor is to

1. Clearly state your goals.
2. Engage your employees, both on where you are headed and in developing ways to get there.
3. Provide resources.
4. Maintain focus with a constant eye on reducing distractions.
5. Balance work loads.
6. Keep a constant focus on the bottom line.

Remember that managing across, up, and down is your responsibility as well, and that building alignment is a key job that, although it may become easy at times, never goes away. Continually building and maintaining alignment, as well as keeping a constant eye on the input needs of resources in the form of tools, people, time, and information to get work done, are critical for the success of any sponsor at any level.

Keys for Change Agents

First, you must identify that you are in the role of the Change Agent. Without this realization, the chance of over- or under-functioning significantly increases. Once you have this realization, know that a key task is to educate and facilitate the work or change. *The area that is most often missed is in the education of the Sponsor of the work.* Most Change Agents easily keep their own boss informed, but they often forget to inform the boss over the resource/Target they are working with. These bosses normally need to know when you will work with their resource, how much time will it take, which emerging issues are critical, how are their people performing (both positively and negatively), the timeline for the work or change, which key moments will need the Sponsor's decision, and any other resource needs you may have. Do this well, and the work or change will become easy. Ignore this, and you may not even know that the Sponsor does not want the work that day; thus, you risk getting into an argument with an employee over a decision that they did not make.

Learn How to Leverage Change

> **Change Agent:** "Boy, the shift 'C' shift leader is so resistant to the new training plan!"
>
> **Consultant:** "Really? Wow, that sounds hard. Tell me what the conversation was like with the shift leader that you had prior to today's meeting when you took the new hires to be trained."
>
> **Change Agent:** "Oh, I haven't talked to him. I just had the meeting with their shift this morning and they were visibly upset in front of the group, plus they didn't allow the new hires to work on their shift yet."
>
> **Consultant:** "What? You mean the shift leader did not know they were getting new trainees today? And you were trying to implement a whole new training program prior to their even knowing?"
>
> **Change Agent:** "Ah, yeah, that is what I mean. Hmmm. Now that you say that, I suppose I could have done a few things differently."

The conversation above is not a composite, but real. In fact, many shift leaders complain about support staff showing up on their shift expecting to do something that uses their employees' valuable time or some other drain on resources. Unexpected visits interrupt the normal daily flow and may impede a critical deliverable. In addition, they do not allow for pre-planning to help the work remain as smooth as possible. It is not surprising or unwarranted that a manager would be upset about such a visit happening when the initiative, training, or process has often been in motion for weeks, months, or sometimes even years.

The ironic thing is that many support staff (change agents who are unaware of their SATA role) still blame the shift leaders or the Targets for complaining and chalk it up to resistance. Sorry, this is not resistance; it is sanity. And it is the key to what I call leveraging change or work.

Your job as a Change Agent is to constantly think through where the work or change will take place and find ways to get the Targets, the Sponsor, and the rest of the system ready. The best way is to actually engage them in the work or change itself. Regardless, educate as to when, what, how, and why the item in question is happening. Then, if there are any questions or concerns, make sure the right Sponsor is having the conversations to get the system aligned.

Best practice for a Change Agent, prior to even arriving, is to have the Initiating Sponsor align Sustaining Sponsors to the work. Project managers, new roles, etc. should never have to introduce their own role to someone whom they must work closely with in order to accomplish a mission-critical task. If that is the case, however, it can be overcome, as long as the Change Agent maintains a systemic focus and knows how to function in a way that helps the system maintain balance and health. State why you think you are there and what you expect to accomplish. Learn about whether or not the Sustaining Sponsor will really be able to sponsor the change properly.

Warning: A Sponsor saying "yes" is not enough unless they also make it a priority, provide resources, and time for completion.

An effective Change Agent must identify uncommitted Sponsors and be willing to do the work of aligning the system. That work normally means a series of conversations with the right Sponsor(s) to help them adjust priorities one way or another. Remember, effective work as a Change Agent here might mean that you find out that the system does not want what you thought you were supposed to be doing. Therefore, you must stop facilitating the change or you will, by definition, become an overfunctioning Change Agent.

Coming back to the example given on page 102, most Change Agents fail when they get a mandate from their boss but then forget about where the work will eventually take place. Thus, when they show up to do the work, neither the Sustaining Sponsor nor the Targets are ready. This is a pay-now-or-pay-later affair. A little time in terms of phone or face-to-face meetings can save a lot of time, money, and employee angst in the long run.

Coaching Your Sponsors

In my role at Alcoa, I became the change management person for the system-wide implementation of Oracle. The task was daunting as we were literally going to implement it in all manufacturing plants across the world, about 40 plants in all. To make matters more difficult, there was an initial impression that we planned to cram it down people's throats without buy-in or input: a method of operating around a large change that rarely works. After coaching the project managers to stop selling the product and start describing it, I helped craft a balanced message that the Business Unit President tweaked and sent out to all employees worldwide. She then followed up with conversations to key players and supported a decision structure I created to ensure balance between IT and the business. Here is the actual letter she sent with the names changed to protect anonymity.

From: Cindy Smith, Typical American Business President
To: All Typical American Business employees
Re: Enterprise Business Solutions Implementation

As a company, we have embarked on a major global IT project that will soon touch each of us. Enterprise Business Solutions (EBS) is the largest non-acquisition expense ever incurred by Alcoa, our parent company. It is an enormous project and a major challenge, even for a company with Alcoa's vast resources.

Beyond installing new enterprise software modules, EBS will also impact our basic business processes. Nearly every process we currently use will be examined and changed. When fully implemented, EBS will affect the way most of us work and do our jobs.

Within CSI, you have already received some early communications on EBS. Mark Howie and Glenn Smith have been appointed the Project Leaders. Glenn is the IT Lead and Mark is the Business Process Lead. With their help and your support, I am assembling a Project team. Planning is underway. Critical timelines are being established. Momentum is quickly building.

My purpose in writing today is to underline that each of us has a major stake in the successful outcome of this project. *This is not an IT project. It is OUR business–critical project–yours and mine.*

Realizing the full benefits of EBS will depend on many factors. Chief among those factors will be effective implementation by the core team–along with employee support, commitment, and hard work at each location. I can guarantee that it will not be easy. To get where we need to go will inevitably require some sacrifice and discomfort on the part of many of you.

There will be bumps in the road ahead. We will need your help to identify those bumps as early on as possible and your active participation in finding the best solutions.

Although there is a project team charged with implementing this project, each of you will also be responsible for the success within your locations. As the project sponsor, I am asking you to fully cooperate with the various implementation teams. I ask that you do everything necessary to achieve optimum success at your locations, as quickly and efficiently as possible.

In the coming days and weeks, you will receive a series of communications from the EBS Lead Team to help you more fully understand the project scope, timelines, and specifics on how you can participate.

CSI's future will depend on how well we pull together as a committed team of 3,500 employees to implement EBS. I am counting on you.

The reason I wanted to show you this is that I find many managers who are not clear what to say or how to say it. Writing an email and letting them put it in their own words is an easy way to help. Most CEOs or managers have plenty going on and like the help. The task of any Change Agent is to help coach the Sponsor in how to lead and communicate the work or change. When you coach the Sponsor do so with your knowledge of the principles outlined in this book on how to align a system and how to create effective change structures. Then make sure they can clearly state the basics: What is the goal in financial terms? What is the completion date? What structures are there for issue resolution and key decisions? Which behavioral expectations ensure results? What time commitments are needed from their employees? How to influence and in what areas? Who really owns the change? How often you will meet? As well as whatever else that the Sponsor thinks is important to convey.

Help managers be honest and not sugarcoat anything. Most employees are pretty smart and can smell inaccurate, untrustworthy messages. A colleague of my father used to say: "When you don't know what to say, the truth is a good place to start." OK, it's a bit too Pollyanna to me but messages which are obviously not true often create mistrust.

A Special Note for External Consultants

If you are an external consultant, you are by definition a Change Agent. No matter if you are an auditor, contractor, engineer, etc., every systemic dynamic mentioned here applies to you. Further, the work you do will be aided by the relationships between the hiring manager and the people he/she wants you to work with (see Chapter 4: Power). If people respect them, you are more likely to be initially seen as worthwhile; if not, you may be set up for a rocky road. Sensitivity to this dynamic is critical. If you ignore it and don't pay attention to SATA, the chance of success is diminished.

Knowing the SATA role of the person who is hiring you is also critical. Are they a Change Agent? Are they an Advocate? Or are they the boss of the people with whom you will work? If you do not know this answer then you likely will fall into the trap of over-functioning and may not even know why you are getting resistance. Worse yet, you could blame it on the people you are working with, rather than use the clear examples from this chapter on how to maneuver and gain alignment in the system.

That is right: it is your job, no matter where you are at in a system, to gain alignment. Blame it on the system and you are stuck in victim thinking.

Key for Targets

You must realize that you have a key role that is most often overlooked in organizations. Your job is to keep the system aligned by letting the Change Agent(s) who come to work with you know if they are out of alignment with the instructions given to you from your Sponsor (your immediate supervisor). Your other key task is to help your Sponsor and Change Agent by letting them know all items in the way of business and goal success. This task can be hard because at times people don't want to hear news that they may consider negative. Your job is to find a way, assuming it is not personally damaging to you, to keep them informed. The reality is you know when things aren't working better than anyone else in the organization.

If you can learn how to keep the system in alignment and guide the change, then the organization will thrive albeit, like the Change Agent, you may not get as much recognition as you deserve. In addition, some Targets have a hard time raising issues with their boss due to authority dynamics (see Chapter 14: Adult Development). Navigating what is real and what is fiction is the task of the Target, as they are in a unique role in the organization, having the least legitimate power.

Keys for Advocates

There are two key tasks for Advocates in all organizations. The first, and most important if you want to be successful, is to identify the right person with whom you have the best opportunity for being heard. If you are an employee and have a small idea related to your work area, it is easy: it is your direct supervisor. If you are in a senior position and you have an idea for a large change which you think would help the entire organization operate more effectively, it then gets trickier. In this case, you must make sure you find the Sponsor over the area you want to change, and you may want to think politically, like whom I should get to support my idea, prior to addressing that Sponsor.

The second task of the Advocate that is the hardest for most to do is to let go when they have presented their idea to the right person and they have said no. This task is often confusing when they have not thought enough about workplace politics and/or found the right Sponsor. An advocate who has been rejected, no matter who rejects them, is often bitter and quick to blame others for their rejection. In fact, most often that Advocate has violated the principles raised above.

Finally, if your idea does get accepted, you may have the additional task of helping the appropriate Sponsor drive the change. If this happens, you must then live by the principles of Change Agent or Target depending on the role you are in after your idea has been accepted. It is important to give up selling your idea, once it has been decided that it will be implemented. Selling will only cause needless tension. Describe it, and let go if anyone has a negative reaction. At this point, your focus must shift to helping it be effectively implemented.

No matter what your situation, the role of Advocate is normally harder to maneuver because most have personal beliefs and a commitment to their ideas beyond the role of Change Agent or Target. To be effective as an Advocate, you must understand your own emotional commitment to your idea and think through the systems implications.

Conclusion

Sponsor Agent Target Advocate has been the most influential theory during my 20-year organization development career. It is the one theory (*which I think is fact more than theory*) that has informed every scenario I have ever been in. I know if I have it straight and operate using its principles, then resistance doesn't exist, polarization fades, true openness happens, and business results are consistently achieved. If you want to succeed, learn and operate using these standards.

Boundary Issues Related to but not the Same as SATA

The ability to distinguish among overworking, over-functioning, micro-managing, alignment issues, and managing is critical to success:

Overworking is about taking on too much responsibility and work. It comes from the inability to draw a boundary by saying "no." Some-times working late hours is necessary but often it is over-compensation for something in the system being out of whack, such as a lack of talent or capabilities, or an inability to spend the time necessary to transfer knowl-edge to the appropriate person. Many bosses don't use enough backbone when spreading tasks. Therefore, they permit overwork by certain em-ployees instead of creating a strategy to balance the workplace. Overwork creates burnout and the lack of knowledge transfer hurts an organiza-tion's ability to learn. Bosses must get engaged at such moments to ensure effective resolution; if left up to the employees, rather than the boss, your workplace will likely suffer.

Another potential root cause of overworking is the fact that in many organizations there is a relative lack of structure or boundaries to help the system learn how to effectively manage certain problems. (See p. 134 on adding structures to solve problems.) In other words, there is an emerging problem(s) with no clear single point of accountability (SPA). Therefore all are held accountable, yet struggling to solve the problem, despite the fact that many employees may have potential solutions. The opposite of holding everyone accountable is having nobody accountable. This situa-tion is a breeding ground for people who tend to take on too much work. Therefore, unless a boss is willing to appoint someone whom Robert

Crosby has termed a "Single Point of Accountability" (SPA), the problem will continue indefinitely. Someone must be appointed SPA in order to solve the problem (see Chapter 7:).

This type of leadership takes backbone and involves, ironically, added tasks that will ultimately reduce the load for all. Many bosses are reluctant to do so, because they have a hard time overseeing the employees who are concerned about extra work. If employees are not provided clear leadership, including creating structures to solve the problems that are leading to overworking, they may find it difficult to get out of its trap.

Micro-managing is giving someone a task, then telling them exactly how to do it when they are capable of figuring it out themselves. It kills initiative and stops thinking from happening below the leadership level. The archetype of this is having a boss standing over your shoulder telling you exactly what to do. Micro-managing is not to be confused with managing new employees who need extra direction and must be told in a step-by-step way what to do and when to call for help, supporting them until they are self-sufficient. Micro-managing is really about capable employees with years of experience and expertise being told how to dot the i's and cross the t's when they obviously don't need the help.

Handing down solutions instead of sharing problems is another subtle form of micro-managing. This often happens when there are problems that are not being solved fast enough for a high-level manager, and instead of getting clear about priorities and dates for solutions to be put in place, the manager imposes a solution. Normally, the solution is good enough, but sometimes its worse than what the employees would have created themselves. Therefore, employee morale suffers. The most upset groups I have ever worked with are those who have had a solution imposed on a problem that they could have solved differently and gotten at least the same results.

When an organization does not spend the time to align its goals from top to bottom in each work group, it increases the probability that these types of boundary issues will recur. Without focused alignment, employees may decide what is important to work on by themselves, which may or may not be best for the business as a whole. In contrast, an alignment process helps ensure that the legitimate authorities have conversations at each level to determine what is best for the business. Leave it up to the employees to figure it out without significant alignment work, and whatever the learned tendencies of the employees are towards over-functioning, overworking, and micro-managing will be heightened.

Managing, on the other hand, is the appropriate act of getting alignment on goals, setting expectations, gaining clarity of task components, effectively working through conflicts of task and people, providing the right resources to get work done (could be time, people, money, tools, information, technical expertise, etc.), and appropriately monitoring the work until completion. Part of managing is making sure each task has a SPA and a clear By-When (completion date): see the keys of creating a culture of accountability on page 117. Due to confusion about authority in most organizations, having a manager ask for a By-When and SPA is often confused with micro-managing. It is not: it is managing and must happen if you want to hit your targets and goals.

A Great Beginning But . . .

A few weeks later. Another meeting at Tim's office. This time Jane came alone.

"Hi, Tim. How are you?"

"Great, Jane, and you?"

"I am pretty good."

"So, tell me. What is the latest? I am so curious."

"Well, since we charted out the players on the project, and identified who the Sustaining Sponsors really are, we've had some great sessions clearing up expectations and re-aligning resources. I now have a fully staffed project team and a timeline complete with tasks."

"Plus, when I go to peoples' offices, they know who I am, and how important the project I am working on is."

"Wow, that sounds great. You had sessions?"

"Yes, Joe brought all the Sponsors in the room, and we talked about the project, its importance, the goals, and the timeline. Those same people then put resources on the project as well as brought up concerns and issues. Lots of those issues we now have plans to fix."

"Wow! That sounds great! But . . . why is it that I sense you are a little down?"

"What? How did you know?"

"Well, usually with a report like yours there would be more smiles and laughs. Am I right?"

"Yeah, I don't really understand, I have a timeline with tasks, yet things are already starting to slip, and some things that are mission-critical. With the clarity Joe provided and the team we assembled, how can that be? Maybe this method just doesn't work."

"Hmmm, yes. Well, I can't answer that without first investigating more. You said you have a timeline, is it with you? Can you share it with me?"

"Sure thing! Let me fire up my laptop," Jane replied.

Jane and Tim then started looking at the timeline and what Tim found was very typical. In fact, it is typical in many organizations. He found a lack of clear accountability within the plan.

Tim started asking questions. "Jane, who is supposed to do this action?"

"Um, well, that is the marketing department."

"And this one?"

"Well, I am not really sure but someone in production."

Tim looked at Jane with a knowing glance. "OK, I see the issue here. Let me talk to you about how to create an accountability culture." Tim then stood up, and went to the whiteboard again.

"You're gonna wear that thing out," Jane joked.

"Yea, it gets some pretty good use!" quipped Tim.

Tim then proceeded to write the words "Single Point of Accountability" and "By-Whens" on the board.

Jane spoke, "I think I get the first point just by reading it, but what exactly is a 'By-When?'"

From here Tim started explaining . . .

◊◊◊

Read Chapter Seven

CHAPTER 7

Accountability

"How do I hold people accountable?"

—countless managers

Introduction

Many managers, ironically, do not know how to hold people accountable and have never been trained in managing people. They either lack the proper structure to do so, or they lack the personal authority (p. 75) to pull it off. While there is no perfect way to ensure happy employees while holding them accountable, there are some basics that many organizations do not have in place. Those basics are clear expectations, which include task-component clarity, single point of accountability, and what we call By-Whens.

Yet, there is more to this in a manager's development. You must be willing and able to confront, and either have legitimate authority (i.e., you do their performance review) or be backed up by those who do have legitimate authority most of the time. If you are in a team-lead or any coordinator-type role, you most likely do not hire or fire the employees you are trying to coordinate. Therefore, you do not have the legitimate formal authority that comes from being someones boss, yet you are expected to act. This type of authority is called "role" authority. In such roles while trying to hold an employee accountable, if you often get vetoed, then the employees will know that they don't really have to listen to you. Therefore, the system is out of alignment. Clarity of authority is the key, however, but not the only ingredient, to accountability. Many managers, with or without legitimate authority, have a hard time appropriately confronting employees in those moments where such action is vital to business success.

Task Component Clarity/Clear Expectations

All tasks need to have maximum clarity so employees will know exactly what, how, and when they are to do it. This is easier if you are a cashier or putting in one bolt on a line, but many are in work environments where they are creating and doing lots of emerging work, so task component clarity can easily get muddled. If you do not work to get maximum clarity of task with your employees or from your boss, then holding your employee accountable is almost impossible.

Single Point of Accountability (SPA)

For each task, action item, or duty there must be one person accountable, a single point of accountability or SPA. Groups or work teams do not do things, people do, and if you have nobody accountable, then good luck knowing whom to hold accountable when things do not get done.

By-Whens

A By-When is a completion date with an added component. By-When ensures communication if dates start to slip. As I stated in the previous section: "It is more than a commitment date, because dates can come and go. It is a *commitment to communicate the status of the task if it starts to slip prior to the completion date.* It accomplishes many things." By-Whens are a key component to helping any organization execute tasks in an ever shifting world. When you can make and follow through with internal By-Whens, you will then provide the same to your external customers as well.

Consequence Management

This can only be effectively done if you have first done work on role clarity, expectations, SPAs, and By-Whens.

> **Manager:** "I told them that this is the last time I will let them get away with that!"
> **Consultant:** "How many times have you told them that?"

Manager: "Oh, about seven!"

Consultant: "Hmmm. Well, I hope you don't tell them eight times! Instead, I want you to learn to apply the consequences."

Consequence management is an important component of accountability. All workplaces have rules and guidelines which dictate how to legitimately hold employees accountable when they do not meet expectations. Rules are not enough; many managers, if not most, have a very difficult time actually exercising their authority. The key to holding people accountable is to have clear expectations, SPAs, and By-Whens, then to use your authority appropriately when needed to actually hold your people accountable. Processes and rules do not hold people accountable; people do. If you rarely, if ever, apply consequence management, then your employees will know that they do not really have to listen to you around rules and expectations. (See p. 75: Personal Authority.)

Role of Leader in Conflict Management

Part of accountability is the setting of clear expectations about how your employees must work together. Most people get along better with some people than others. All leaders must pay attention to their employees and intervene if tense moments persist long enough that effective work is not being done. It is the duty of the manager to ensure effective employee interactions and to find ways to constructively manage moments that are not working. Leaders must learn how to use their personal and legitimate authority to ensure both that the immediate conflict gets resolved and that plans for how to manage similar situations in the future are put into place. This applies both to individuals and groups in conflict. Many managers are unaware that how they deal with workplace conflict is a choice, and in fact, is more about behaviors *they are or are not doing*, than about the employees under them who are in the conflicts themselves. Effectively resolving conflict is a choice that most do not realize they have. (See Appendix L of *CCIO* for a detailed account of how to help two employees work through a conflict.)

What Am I Missing?

About an hour later . . .

Tim asked another question, "So, Jane, how often do you meet with the people on the project?"

"Meet?" said Jane tilting her head to the side.

Tim continued, "Yes, to work issues and to follow-up on tasks."

Jane answered, "I occasionally hold a meeting but I don't have a set time. People on the project have so much to do that I don't want to bother them."

"Hmmm, this also could be a problem," said Tim.

Jane spoke up, "You know, it seems so hit-and-miss and chaotic around here, that I often ask myself, what am I missing?"

"Yes," said Tim. "This may seem odd but clarity of sponsorship is not enough. Now that you are working to clarify sponsorship and are seeming to make real headway, let me introduce another concept: structure."

"I suggest setting predictable and logical routines that effectively engage the people on your project to solve the emerging issues and problems. Then, strategically involve other key people throughout the organization, at critical junctures, on the specific issues with which they need to be involved."

"Now that you are clear about the need for an SPA for key roles and tasks, the next step is creating a sustainable structure for your work."

With structure, as with many things, you can have too much or too little.

Here are a few of the critical dimensions to think about as you decide what is best for your unique situation.

And with that, Tim went back to the whiteboard to draw another continuum. He then wrote the words "too much" and "too little" on either end. In the middle he wrote "the sweet spot."

◊◊◊

Read Chapter Eight

CHAPTER 8

Structure

Introduction

The Organization Theory presented in this chapter holds the key to changing your organization in a balanced, positive way. The solution is not the "next best way" to talk, to problem solve, or to organize. All those things can help, but all will fail unless the people, your people, are led with clarity and your organization is aligned.

Alignment and clarity happen one conversation at a time, work group by work group, layer by layer. Authority exists in every organization. When you methodically and consistently gain clarity throughout your system, employees will know their boundaries and be able to move with ease and determination. True culture change is not possible without having clarity on the topics presented here. You may start moving your organization in a new direction, but you will not be able to sustain that momentum until you are truly aligned.

Freedom and Structure

Freedom is a funny word. Many see it as the "ability to do whatever I want, whenever I want." Yet that is not freedom. That is anarchy. The roots of Organization Development in the USA came out of World War II and were heavily influenced by the types of governments that were operating at the time. Kurt Lewin, the father of Social Psychology, and the person most associated with the OD movement in the USA, fled Hitler and was highly aware of the dangers of extreme styles of governance. He applied his experience directly to organizations and had great success as a practitioner by helping balance freedom and structure. John Dewey and Lewin both believed and deeply understood that there is no freedom without structure. Most workplaces lack this understanding and, therefore, create environments stuck in one extreme or the other. Both Dewey and Lewin say the ability to lead in this new way, which is in the middle between too permissive and too autocratic, is, in fact, a learned behavior. They both claim it must be taught to each generation of leaders. Achieving the balance between the extremes takes hard work and persistence, and can be lost in a heartbeat if a high-level leader who manages from either extreme take the reins.

During a recent leadership and emotional intelligence training, employees of one business lined up on a continuum of authority in their system. Authority has two extremes, from very permissive to very autocratic, so those two extremes were the basis of the continuum.

The first question that employees lined up on was how it was in their organization prior to the sale to the new corporate ownership. At that time, the company was a family-owned business with 400 employees, where most decisions were made from the owners. The lineup surprised me a bit as employees ranged all along the continuum from permissive to autocratic. The stories about how they were managed differed mostly from where they were in management or on the floor.

The second continuum represented how it was today since the new manager took the reins. (He had utilized most of the principles of this book.) Again, a surprise to me: most employees clumped towards the autocratic side. The surprise really came when they talked about why.

Story after story were about how people were being held accountable to their work and how it was better than it had been. They talked about how clear decision-making was, how they now knew what was expected of them, and of others, and how they actually had appropriate consequences if work did not get accomplished. The reasons so many went towards the autocratic side turned out to be because they were finally all being held accountable and, ironically, it related more to structure than autocratic decision making.

The Role of Structure

Clarity of Authority is essential for effectiveness, but it is not enough. In other words, just because you are aware of and live within the boundaries of SATA, or you spend time clarifying and pushing down decision-making authority, it will not necessarily lead to better business results.

In order to create an effective workplace, *you must also have clear structures beyond the frame of authority* to ensure an efficient flow of information. Such structures ensure effective information flow of items such as clarity of day-to-day task components, decision making, strategy and tactics, and interfaces throughout the organization.

Structure is an important part of what helps leaders and employees stay appropriately engaged, in order to achieve bottom-line results. Non-engagement of all key employees for day-to-day activities, critical tasks, problem solving, key initiatives, or projects cannot be optional or your organization's success is left to chance. With such clear evidence that effective structure leads to high-level functioning, why leave it to chance?

However, maintaining effective structures is a commitment and an ongoing task in and of itself. To do so requires the ability to use your authority to hold people accountable (see p. 75: "Personal Authority").

Clarity of authority is the foundation of effective structures. The process to clarify authority is an educational one. SATA must be used strategically to understand which employees need to get aligned to what goals, initiatives, and projects. Decision making must be clarified and applied, situationally, to all employees to ensure appropriate empowerment and speed of action. If Dewey and Lewin are right, and clearly I believe they were, then managing from the middle is hard work and must be learned by each generation. The task of education never ends. Stop it, and you risk slipping into either extreme of "too autocratic" or "too permissive."

Structure should be based on the unique situations within your business. You can have too much or too little. Too much structure can handcuff an organization by imposing so many rules that employees stop thinking for themselves. Too little structure creates chaos as employees miss out on the critical info they need to do their job.

Below is a continuum of structure.

This continuum applies to all organizations and can be used to find a balance in your current situation. Use it to analyze your current structures and adjust them so they ensure effective business functioning, engage the right employees, promote information flow, clarify task components, enable quick and efficient decision making and, ultimately, achieve better bottom-line results.

Figure 17 Structure Continuum

What follows are some common structures to be aware of and to manage effectively based on your unique situation. The list is by no means all-inclusive; other new structures may be identified and created. The key is balance: if you are not getting business results, ask if it is from too little or too much structure. Then adjust accordingly. Make small adjustments and follow up effectively (see Chapter 10: Follow-Up). Do not go from one extreme to another, but make small changes until the system is working. Balancing authority and creating the right amount of structure is the key for effective employee engagement and business results.

Meetings

Number and length—If your work group must be coordinated to get their work done, then you must have some meetings. The more complex, the more important the meeting is. It is critical for everyone to be on the same page at the same time; not meeting at all adds unnecessary risk to workplace productivity. "How often?" should be the only question: never is unwise; every day is probably too much. Most work teams or departments with multiple functions need to meet at least once a month or so. Meeting agendas should include what is or is not working as well as critical issues that need addressing. Not all have to be formal: some may well be stand-up meetings of 5 to10 minutes where key players gather to make sure they are on the same page.

There should also be meetings between departments or functions who must support each other to ensure the business is running properly. Again, if it is critical that you work well together to ensure business success, you cannot afford to leave it to chance by never meeting. Instead, create a structured meeting to focus on cross-functional needs and adjust it until you achieve results.

Meeting effectiveness—If meetings you run are not working and you are not getting positive results, do not blame the fact that you are meeting as the problem. Perhaps you need new strategies for running a more effective meeting. Small adjustments should get the meeting working well for you. Deciding to go from poorly run meetings to not having them at all is an injustice. Instead, learn how to create structured meetings that work, wasting neither your employees nor your time (see *Walking the Empowerment Tightrope*, p. 42, Action Idea: Improve Meetings).

Shift-change meetings—Manufacturing facilities generally work in shifts. In most cases there are shift change meetings to close out the outgoing shift, prepare the incoming shift, and ensure effective coordination of critical issues that need extra attention. In most shift-change meetings, employees learn what they will work on today as well hear updates, such as what machines are down, what current problems are being worked on, daily work instructions, and staffing. These meetings are either helping or not. Create an effective structure to follow at such meetings to ensure they are as productive as possible. Here are some items to consider.

- Can the employees hear each other?
- Do the employees repeat instructions given to them to ensure understanding?
- Can employees raise issues?
- Is there a structure that ensures dialogue?
- Is there enough time to exchange detailed information with the outgoing shift?

Some of these items may seem obvious, but when I was asked to observe shift-change meetings in one plant, I could not hear a word the manager said. Yet, none of the employees spoke up. Most manufacturing plant floors are loud, so make sure you are not duplicating that experience. Structure your shift-change meetings to include employee interaction around instructions, raising of issues, learning from the previous shift, and ensure that all can clearly hear what is being said. Tap into and utilize the full potential of the worker knowledge of your shift employees.

Clear Single Point of Accountability (SPA)

Simply stated, single-point accountability means having one person responsible for one job. There are two types of SPA referenced here. One is role SPA such as a project manager or employee who is tasked with a major cross-functional initiative. The other use of SPA is specific to individual actions: one person responsible for one task. Either there is one person accountable, or there is not. Clear single point of accountability is a critical structure: utilize it to define who isaccountable for every task that is important for the business. I have seen organization after organization get upset, because people were not being "responsible," while at the same time allowing lack of clarity of an SPA. Whenever all are responsible, then no one is responsible. Confusion will reign.

Clarity of SPA sounds simple but it is not, due to several factors.

One, there is a tendency in organizations to think in terms of groups rather than of people. When assigning actions or tasks, some allow a department or work group to be the SPA. People perform tasks, not departments. If you allow for this, you increase confusion about whom to speak with about any given assignment. Having to seek out whoever is actually doing the task increases waste in the system.

Two, many tasks are done by multiple people working together and, in those cases, it is easy to think that you should put all names in the SPA column. Do not fall for this. An SPA is by definition one person and, if you break this rule, you will add confusion about who is accountable and thus responsible for status updates. If needed, add a "work with" column to your accountability sheets to gain clarity of whom the SPA must work with, but do not break the principle of Single Point of Accountability.

Finally, people often get assigned responsibilities who are not in the right department or area to be held accountable. If you put a shift leader in charge of replenishing spare parts for the line, or a give a lean expert responsibility for doing day-to-day tasks in a particular department, you are letting the employees, who should do the work, off the hook. Countermeasures to solve particular problems are acceptable but quickly fix the root of the problem and make sure you put in place the right SPA. Analyzing who is the right SPA is an ongoing task that needs to continue until the business is functioning well and you are getting commensurate results.

SPA for Initiatives

If you have more than one person working on an initiative, it needs to be clear who the SPA or point person is. This is not about power or abuse; it is about clarity. Who stays on top of things and bird-dogs tasks? Who do you go to in order to learn what is happening with the task and overall progress of the initiative? If you allow five or six people to work on something yet no one person has Single Point Accountability, you will introduce more potential chaos than you need.

Clear Goals

Clarity of goals is key to helping your employees understand why the tasks they are doing matter, how they connect with the overall direction of the business, and which areas they need to help improve on to reach them. Robert Crosby's "Rainbow Model of Goals" outlines three types of goals: bottom line, work process, and human factors (see p. 23). All employees are using work processes and executing tasks that directly relate to the bottom line, yet most have limited comprehension of the real metrics they are working towards and which processes, related to bottom-line goals, they need to improve.

You increase employee engagement by spending the time to help them make the connection between their job's tasks and the organization's success. Recent neurological research suggests that the neocortex literally shuts down if employees are unaware of why they are doing their task, and how it contributes to the organization's success. The neocortex is the thinking center of the brain. It is responsible for helping people process information, overall brain functioning, and the analysis needed to contribute ideas for improvement. That scenario literally means that the amygdala (fear center) and the reactive parts of the emotional brain will have a larger impact on employee behavior.

Beyond the distinction between bottom-line and work process goals is ensuring *balance* in your bottom-line goals, as well as the ability to measure them. Increasing production does not help unless you simultaneously improve quality. Balance is key.

Creating clear goals sounds easy, but for most it is a major challenge. The distinction between an action, a standard, and a goal is often confused.

Here is a quick way to think about it with an example coming from sales.

Example of an action—Create a new service standard for customer requests.

Example of a standard—Reply to customer requests within one hour.

Example of a goal—Reach new customer service standard 95 percent of the time.

Make sure each goal selected is critical for effective business functioning. The example given is a work process goal that is intended to focus the employees on quicker responses to the customer. Once any goal is created, of course, there needs to be a way to track it. From there, the employees who are to be measured by the goal must learn and understand it. There also needs to be a clear process that engages them to raise any issues in the way of success and, of course, in developing actions to overcome those issues.

Decision Clarity

Decision clarity is another structure that can and should be worked throughout your workplace. Many employees are in situations in which they have to wait for decisions, which they could have easily decided by themselves. *Yet, they are not granted the authority to do so.* It takes time to clarify decision making but, in the long run, if it is done well you will increase your speed and efficiency. (Chapters 12 and 13 act as guides for applying this in your organization.)

Expectations/Role Clarity

Every employee has expectations which are either clear or fuzzy. The goal: scientifically verifiable expectations so everyone knows what to do, and what not to do. The key to this is behavioral specifics (see Chapter 4 of *Fight, Flight, Freeze*).

Here are some examples:

Fuzzy—"I need you to be responsive to sales."

Clear—"I need you to answer questions from sales within two hours of them making an inquiry. If you cannot find the answer, you must call and tell them within those two hours. Then I need you to make and meet the next deadline you create with them."

Fuzzy—"I need you to be a better team player."

Clear—"I need you to hear and fulfill requests without saying, 'Here we go again?' or 'Aye, aye, Sir!' I also need you to complete requests on time or negotiate if that time frame will not work."

Methods

To help ensure consistent and effective behavior in an organization, it is important to utilize a set of *methods: careful, organized plans which control the way something is done.* In other words, a method outlines a process that is a consistent and reliable way to do something.

Here are some examples:

- Problem-solving techniques
- Toll-gate process for projects
- Software development processes
- Testing techniques

You may ask: What is the best method? The answer is the one that works best in your unique situation. Since each workplace is different, you must explore and find the method that suits your needs. Then, adapt it to your unique situation. Some methods are better than others. What is more important is that you find a consistent way to produce effective outcomes and then employ whichever you choose appropriately.

Methods work best when they are clearly sponsored, the organization around them is aligned, and they are adapted to your unique situation. Once you do that and include the right people, then you must have effective follow-through until results are consistently achieved. The problem with most methods: they are implemented in a vacuum with a lack of clear sponsorship and follow-through. It then becomes easier to blame the method for not working than to reflect on how the organization is functioning around it. Slight tweaks may be enough to get the method back on track. Clarity of methods is critical, especially when combined with sponsorship and alignment.

A few warnings—One, I have seen many organizations develop solid methods yet go *overboard in their use*. In other words, now that we have this method, our new hammer, we should use it on everything, because they all look like nails. Do your best to not let this happen. Two, I have also seen organizations that create a toll-gate process or a software development process that quickly become *too cumbersome*. It is important to give guidelines to help the business effectively think through stages and talk to the various departments. Yet, there is a temptation to let the process manage the people, rather than vice versa. Therefore, it is easy to have toll-gate processes consume too much time and stall projects for non-business critical reasons or software development processes that spin the developers in circles. The goal should be to stay focused on your business outcomes and use your methods as a means to the end, rather than as an end in itself.

Follow-up

In *Cultural Change in Organizations,* I wrote: "If you check off a list of tasks and expect that to get you to your end game, then you are missing the point. Tasks are merely hypotheses about what will solve a problem. Follow-up is the process of driving tasks to completion and making sure you obtain your stated objective."

In reality, many start initiatives or develop lists of actions, but few actions are followed up well. Some allow statements like "It's OK" or "It's all good" to be allowed as follow-up and then move on. Effective follow-up has two components. First, did you do the task that you said you would do up to a high standard? Second, did you get the intended results? Both components must be evaluated in order to know if you chose the right solution, and if it solved the problem for which it was intended. Poor follow-up can hide many things, such as ineffective implementation practices, resource constraints, and priority conflicts. If you keep creating lists yet tasks are slipping, conversations about alignment and importance are likely not happening. Managers with the mentality "We must get it all done" will miss key insights into their group if they do not effectively follow-up. They will also most likely not achieve their goals.

Leadership is about following tasks till problems are solved. If you start many tasks but never complete any, you are just spinning your wheels.

Make sure you create clear structures and guidelines for follow-up that get incorporated into each meeting and work group (see Chapter 10).

Clarity of Authority

A partner to decision-making, clarity of authority is about knowing my boundaries of authority. It is being clear about who my boss is, who my subordinates are, and what authority I have at any given time. In matrixed or cross-functional workplaces, it is key when conflicting priorities surface. Clear authority allows you to create guidelines and boundaries aligned with what is best for the business. If there is no clear structure to break impasses between employees or departments, then it will likely lead to scenarios where decisions are made by a "test of wills" versus what is best for the organization as a whole.

Conflict Management

Effective organizations have structures to help deal with differences between departments and employees. One such structure is to develop a cadre of employees who are trained and skilled at third-party conflict resolution. The first step is to be honest about the reality: conflict exists within your organization as, of course, it does in all. The second step is to set boundaries and expectations around how they are to be resolved. Finally, managers must have the personal authority to insist that it happens and that it is followed up until there is resolution. Most organizations have departments or people who are not working together well enough so that productivity is being hurt, yet few managers have the backbone, personal authority, or structure in place to effectively deal with it. There are well documented ways to help effectively manage workplace conflict (see Appendix L of *CCIO*: "Third Party Conflict Resolution").

By-Whens

By-Whens, clear commitment dates for achieving a task, are negotiated by those involved in tasks. It is more than a commitment date, because dates can come and go. It is a commitment to communicate the status of the task if it starts to slip prior to the completion date. It accomplishes many things. First, it keeps everyone on the same page of what is happening. Second, it establishes clear communication links. Finally, it is a key to accountability. Since it is about keeping key players in the loop, by-whens are about respecting all others in the organization so that they can do their tasks with clarity as well.

Choosing to Add or Delete Structure

The decision to add or delete structure is situational and ongoing. There are many factors to keep in mind, such as business size (number of employees), complexity, and results. Let us take meetings as an example. Certainly, if you are in 12 three-hour meetings a week, there is too much structure going on. On the other hand, if you are leading a group that has many complexities and never meets to get on the same page, you have too little. You can, and should, apply the same kind of thinking to the various structures in your situation. (For a questionnaire to assess your group, see Appendix C.)

Many organizations have problems with processes and try to quickly regain control by adding steps or taking away and reassigning duties. Adding extra sign-offs and batching computer inputs are examples of such fixes. The problem comes when temporary fixes get set in stone: the crisis structure is, therefore, left in place indefinitely. Oftentimes, such counter-measures hide the roots of the problem, such as when employees need to talk prior to a contract but do not, or when a few employees make inputs incorrectly. It is OK to gain control if things are out of control. All organizations must do this from time to time, but the goal should be to become as functional as possible while staying responsive to the customers' needs.

Instead of maintaining a system put in place in time of crisis, revisit it by doing a thorough problem-solving process, and create a better system that honors the current needs of the organization. Make sure that you then give your employees the training, tools, and resources to be successful. This involves time, trust, training, personal authority, and persistence.

A Major Glitch

A few weeks later . . .

"Hi, Jane. How are you?"

"Don't ask," said a dejected Jane.

"What?" Tim said, surprised and a bit worried.

"Honestly, Tim, I just came today to vent, it's so terrible. I cannot stand it. Not that I haven't seen it before."

"Terrible?" Tim said.

"Yes, our IT Engineering department has ground to a halt and they are fighting with the Product Managers, again!"

"Again?" replied a surprised Tim. "But you have only been here a few months."

"Yes, but this one happens everywhere," replied Jane. "I have seen it a million times."

"Hmmm. Tell me more."

"Well, John Snyder is implementing our latest software at one of our key clients and they have run into a major problem that can't seem to be fixed. The software won't work right and when that happens, most companies, ours is no exception, start subtly infighting. The product managers blame the engineers and vice versa. My problem is I need those engineers to be working on our software or we will start seeing delays," Jane said, as she sank in her seat. "I wish I could just wave a magic wand and have this problem go away."

"Hmmm. So how can I help?"

"That's just it," said Jane. "I don't know how you can . . .

"Hey!" said Jane, a light had just gone on. "Would you be willing to have a conversation with John?"

"John," said Tim. "Well, OK. Do you think he really wants my advice? After all, a wise person once said: 'The only real vice is advice,' especially if it's unwanted."

"Hmmm. I am not sure," Jane replied, "but I could ask. No harm in that, right?"

"True," Tim said with a smile.

◊◊◊

Sure enough, Jane called John and, within minutes, John was at the door eager to talk, seemingly pleased to be here. Yet, he also looked quite frazzled.

"Hi, John!" Jane said.

"Hey," John replied.

"Hi, John. I am Tim."

"Oh, hi," John responded. "Jane keeps talking you up. How are you?"

"Well, I am great. The question is: How are you?"

"Terrible," John said.

"Really? What is happening?"

"Well, I think I got everybody upset at me: the engineers, the product managers, and the client. The adjustments we are making to the software during implementation are not working. I even have Sally, the Sr. Vice President of Product Management involved. When she gets involved you know it's a problem."

"So what's going on?" Tim inquired.

John continued, "My client has a problem. As we put in one fix other problems then arise. This client system has 20 different sites and I am working with a representative they assigned to oversee it. Each change we make to correct a problem for one site is creating problems at others. The software engineers are quite upset. It seems like more of them are getting involved. It is becoming a problem within the whole organization. Then Sally swoops down and starts demanding things and it becomes the same old Product Manager versus Software Engineer battle. Yet, this one has remained and the problems are not getting fixed and the client is also getting frustrated."

"Hmmm. Can you tell me a little more about the situation?" asked Tim.

"OK," said John. "We're replacing the software for a large percentage of our carriers that are still using the old platform, which doesn't really integrate well with all of our other platforms. I am leading a project that we are calling an upgrade, but really it's a replacement of one software with another and it impacts a lot of carriers. Right now we are trying to implement a major client that has about 20 carrier sites across several states, so it gets to be complicated."

"Hmmm. And who are you working with to identify the problems in the client system?" Tim asked.

"They have a super-user appointed who, up to this point, has been great. On this one, however, we seem to have hit a wall," John replied.

"And you are using the same platform across five states? Are you trying to have it exactly the same?" Tim asked with concern in his voice.

"That is the charge from Ed," John said, somewhat dejected.

"Ed? Is that the same Ed I know?" Tim said with a smile.

"One and the same!" replied Jane.

"John," said Tim, "there are two concepts that, I think, could really help you work through this maze. One involves broadening who you are talking with, and the other involves developing a strategy from your end, with the right leadership support to allow for enough flexibility per state. I would be happy to share them if you want to learn more?"

"Um. . . .YES!!!" Both Jane and John spoke in unison.

"OK, this one involves getting the system—by that I mean the workplace—aligned to work a slightly different way and probably requires a conversation with Joe, Ed, and Sally. I would be happy to be part of that conversation if you want."

"What? Hang on, Tim. I can't get those people talk to each other!" said a concerned John.

Tim replied, "Hmmm. To align, people have to have difficult conversations."

Jane, you seem to have Joe's ear. Do you think you can help John here pull it off?"

"Tim," said Jane. "I know there is a lot of pressure to succeed. I think, if I need to, I can present the business problem to get that conversation. But what would we talk about?"

"That is what I want to teach you," said Tim. "These two concepts, together, will help you develop a strategy to learn about the right problems from the right people at each site and to set some boundaries which will help you succeed. Once that happens, your software engineers will easily make the software adjustments that will work at each site."

John spoke up, "The Software Engineers are great when they have clear requirements and problems to solve, but so far we have been guessing."

"I get it," said Tim. "The first concept is called *adapt/adopt* and the second is about *workplace knowledge*." From there, Tim went to the whiteboard.

Jane chuckled "Hee hee! John, get used to this. Tim loves that board."

"Yes," replied Tim, "a wise man once said: 'There is nothing so practical as a good theory.' So I like it when I have one to give that is applicable. This board gets a lot of use."

◊◊◊

Read Chapter Nine
and Appendix I of *Cultural Change in Organizations*

CHAPTER 9

Workplace Knowledge

All organizations have an abundance of underutilized knowledge for solving problems while racing towards the bottom line. In this small but critical section, I outline the types of knowledge that exist within all organizations to help you think through who needs to be involved and in which situations.

Manager Knowledge—A manager's knowledge is cumulative. It takes time to learn how to manage any department, plant, or group because all are comprised of humans and all are unique. That is why all managers learn about how to manage their unique system as they do their job. Some have had the luxury of being trained in theories of behavioral dynamics, but mostly they are promoted into their positions due to their technical expertise, their job performance, and/or because they can do both things without creating waves.

The more managers are in the position, the more they understand their position and the organization within which they are managing. The unique position of being a manager gives you a perspective of the department, plant, or system that is different from the viewpoint of those doing the work. Therefore, it has the advantage and potential of being "above the trees." By stepping back, managers can see how all employees are working together and make strategic tweaks intended to ensure successful business output.

Manager knowledge is the most utilized in organizations. The primary attempt to solve most problems involves gathering managers and having them generate and impose solutions.

Technical Expertise Knowledge—The second most utilized knowledge in organizations is called technical expertise. It involves professionals with expertise in machines, processes, methodologies, etc. They developed their expertise through combining training, education, and years of experience in their field, and are often called on to give expert advice on how to solve issues.

The unique position of a technical expert is that they have focused on one or a series of items specifically related to their area. They can often give "the answer" about things that managers and other workers cannot.

Worker Knowledge—This knowledge is the least utilized in most organizations. Worker knowledge is the knowledge that comes from doing the task or job day-in and day-out. While workers often do not know how processes, people, or departments are connected, they do possess a knowledge that no manager or technical expert can ever fully have. They are first to experience dysfunction in the workplace created by misalignment, poor processes, practices, or broken equipment.

All workers know when there are problems in their organization. They know when machines go down, when materials don't arrive, and when new ideas won't work and why. They also know potential issues that could hurt success and where things have gone wrong in the past. They know this by living it day-by-day, rather than by theory. Although this can sometimes create a myopic view for employees, especially if they have often not been heard while watching initiatives fail, it is a viewpoint that is critical to success.

The distinction of the types of knowledge in organizations is important because *when any business is trying to solve a major problem, they must utilize a balance of knowledge.* The knowledge that I find missing most often in major problem solving is worker knowledge.

"Let's make sure we only have a few people in the room,
so we can manage the conversation."

—countless managers

One common reason for not utilizing worker knowledge is the lack of training on how to structure events to make sure all voices get heard and the conversation does not descend into chaos. Many managers have brought a large number of people together, applied no meeting structure, and gotten nowhere, with some speaking in ways that upset others. "Too many people in the room" is then blamed as "the problem."

Sorry, the problem was you did not think through the design of the meeting and you do not know how to structure an event so that it can be productive, no matter how many are in the room. Instead of restricting input of worker knowledge, learn how to structure large groups in order to solve problems. Make sure you include a balance of managerial, technical, and worker knowledge when solving key problems, so that you are able to solve at the root level and to institute solutions which will actually work.

On large-scale initiatives or critical projects, we routinely facilitate groups of 40 to 100 people in the room. We do so by having a clear structured approach and often use multiple facilitators. Once you teach a group a process a few times, then they will begin to self-facilitate using the social technology they have learned. The meetings referenced consisted of at least 50 percent of the people who do the work. Thus, the worker knowledge was well utilized and key to solving their issues. (The basic guidelines for such a session are outlined in Appendix N of *Culture Change in Organizations*. When structured according to the principles in that Appendix, and followed up diligently according to the principles in Chapter 10, the business results are almost unbelievable.)

Worker knowledge routinely gets forgotten in even smaller changes where only a few people do the work. I worked with a manufacturer who wanted to improve their spare part on-time delivery in order to capture market share. Their current on-time delivery rate was 47 percent. The belief was that if they improved their performance to a reasonable rate of 75 percent, they could increase sales by $7 million per year. When I arrived to do the improvement activity the day before the event,

I asked them who was in it. The response? They told me about five managers, all over areas where the work would take place. They were attempting to solve the problem without input from the people making the parts or taking the orders.

I coached them on the importance of balancing the participants and including the knowledge of the workers on the floor. They were hesitant but agreed to do so. The next day as issues were raised at each step of the process, it became clear how critical these people were. Critical info would have been missed such as:

From the person making the parts—"I used to make the parts, log them in the computer, and put them away. Now I make the parts, hand in a piece of paper, they get put away at the end of the week, and it sometimes takes us literally days to find them. Please let me do it myself again."

From the customer service person—"When a customer asks a question, I have to find whomever I can to get answers. Sometimes it takes me literally days to get back to the customer for even simple requests. Please give me a dedicated person who will get me answers within an hour or so."

Workers always know what is not working, yet they do not often have a clear path to share it, and are often unheard. I did not make up those examples; they are real. In fact, once they created clear strategies to solve the issues raised, and drove them to completion, they reached 95 percent on-time delivery, and did in-fact capture $7 million in additional sales. If they would not have included the worker knowledge, they would have missed some critical problems to solve, and the chance to motivate their workers at the same time. Most employees want to be part of solving the problems that have been a thorn in their sides for years.

Why Are Things Still Choppy?

Two weeks later, Jane came back to Tim's office.

"Hi, Jane! How are you?"

"I am pretty good," said Jane. Yet, her voice betrayed her answer.

"Hmmm. Why am I skeptical?" replied Tim.

"Well, OK. I am still struggling but at least that last disaster was averted."

"Really, that's great news. Can you fill me in?" said Tim eagerly.

"Yeah, sure," said Jane. "Once you talked to us about the importance of utilizing worker knowledge, it became blindingly obvious to John what he needed to do. He then asked his client to get employees who do the work—in this case the carriers themselves—from locations within each state that is implementing so that they can raise their own unique issues.

At the same time, I filled in Joe on your concept of *adapt and adopt* and he immediately got it. From there, he conducted a high-level meeting to develop more logical boundaries for changes to the software during implementations which include branчces that cross states. Then he had an emergency meeting with the leadership over the product managers and the software engineers to gain clarity of what we can adapt and what must be adopted in the new software platform.

In fact, he first talked to Sally and Ed together, then they had an expanded meeting with the right people involved to share the boundaries. Joe was wise here. He presented the boundaries as a first draft and wanted to know where they hit the mark, missed the mark, and needed small tweaks. This despite some pushback from both Sally and Ed.

After that, Joe gave people a few days to think about it. Then, they reconvened and decided, with Joe making the final call. Not everyone got what they wanted, but clarity was evident and a path forward with the client was achieved.

It was amazing, surprisingly fast, and after Ed and a few others raised their objections to not having a completely vanilla system, they came to a very clear—and I must say very practical—solution to use going forward. In fact, it will definitely help me and I have added a meeting to my timeline to do the same thing prior to starting the implementation phase.

But that is not the best part. Once we did this, we had some meetings with the leaders at the client system to explain it, and make sure it fit within what they want. They 'bought in' immediately and committed to driving the expectations within their system.

Afterwards, we met with an expanded set of end users from each state and started by clarifying what could be changed and what cannot, and then developed software adjustments to be tailored slightly differently per state. The engineers made the adjustments and the client is very happy.

So your two observations were right on and very helpful!"

◇◇◇

"Wow. That's great to hear," said Tim. "Yet . . . you still have a long face."

"Yes, because in my project things still seem choppy," said Jane, frustrated.

"Choppy?" asked Tim.

"Yeah, well," Jane continued somewhat happily, "I actually think I have a decent structure and I meet regularly." She paused and then the long look came back on her face, "Yet, actions are still not getting accomplished. I mean, a lot do, but others do not. It just seems like such a struggle."

"Hmmm," said Tim, with an inquisitive look on his face. "I know that we talked a long time about structure. Maybe it's time we go deeper into the critical components of what I call 'follow-up.'"

"Oh," said Jane, "I know all about that. After all, I have regular meetings."

"Hmmm," said Tim. "Just in case, let's review the important elements needed to ready the system for successful follow-up."

"The system?" said Jane, seemingly surprised by the use of these words.

"Yes, the system," Tim continued. "Many, if not most, in the role of project manager or change agent, like you are in, *miss* the *critical function of education* that leads to success. Preparing and aligning the organization to ensure solid follow-up is part of that function."

Jane chuckled.

Tim, surprised, said, "Did I say something funny?"

"Not really, but I was just thinking how much you love that white-board, and there you go again."

"Hmmm. You know me too well," Tim said with a smile. "OK, this is the 'Arc of Follow-Up.'"

◊◊◊

Read Chapter Ten

CHAPTER 10

Follow-Up

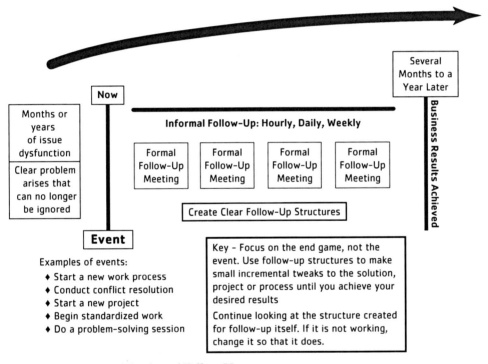

Figure: 18 *The Arc of Follow-Up*

Follow-up is the act of driving actions and commitments after they are created. To do it effectively, you must track the action until it is completed and make sure it solves the problem that it was intended to solve. It sounds simple but, in fact, this seemingly simple act is often overlooked, underdone, avoided, or even somehow compromised.

There is an unacknowledged crisis of follow-up in most organizations. Meeting after meeting, people set actions in place and, rarely if ever, are they reviewed to see if the tasks actually were completed, not to mention whether they solved the problems they were intended to. This appendix includes some basic principles to break that cycle. If a task is important enough to commit to, drive it until completion and see if you obtain the desired results. From there, decide what to do next. Do not fall into the trap of committing to an action, not following up, and then wondering what is going on with it, or worse, forgetting about it. That is a recipe for a stuck workplace.

A common follow-up cycle in many organizations is represented below.

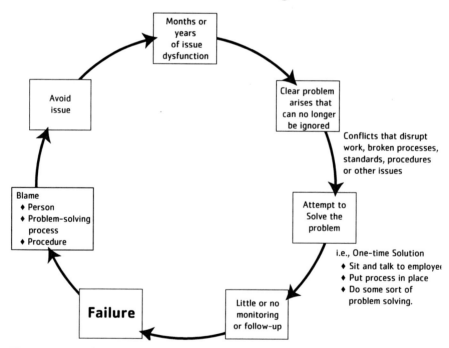

Common Organization Cycle
Related to initiatives and change

- Months or years of issue dysfunction
- Clear problem arises that can no longer be ignored

Conflicts that disrupt work, broken processes, standards, procedures or other issues

- Attempt to Solve the problem

i.e., One-time Solution
- ♦ Sit and talk to employee
- ♦ Put process in place
- ♦ Do some sort of problem solving.

- Little or no monitoring or follow-up
- Failure
- Blame
  - ♦ Person
  - ♦ Problem-solving process
  - ♦ Procedure
- Avoid issue

Figure 19 Dysfunctional Cycle of Follow-Up

Fundamentals of Follow-Up Check List

The first step of follow-up is to get clear about what you are following up. Below is a list of elements needed to create an effective checklist.

- **Action List Created:** When you create an action, write it on a list. It must be in Excel or Word or any program that can be emailed.
- **Minimum Requirements Met for Action List (see Figure 20):**
  - *Who* is to do the action (Single Point of Accountability or SPA)? Never assign an action to a group. Why? Because groups are not accountable, people are. Actions assigned to groups increase the odds of confusion and finger pointing.
  - *What* is the action? (It must be written clearly with action words.)
  - *By-When.* A completion date with an added communication component (see p. 118).
- **Each Action Clarified with the Person Who Is Doing It:** The day after the list is created, circle back to those who are SPA and make sure they understand what the action is and the completion date. This can be a quick 2 to 5 minutes stand-up meeting.
- **Actions Checked with SPA for Resource Problems:** When checking for clarity, also ask if they have the appropriate time, tools, training, and authority needed to do the task. If the answer is no, then make the adjustments so that they can be successful. That might mean giving the task to another person or clearing things with their boss so they have the right resources to accomplish it. Checking for resource problems is a continuous task.
- **Action List Used as a Communication Tool:** Share it with those impacted and with others who have tasks on the same list, to get clarity of the action and updates of status. Use an overhead projector and talk through who is doing what periodically.

Who (SPA)	What	By When
Phil	Provide critical list of parts—top "50"—that guarantees 5-working-day delivery. Give list to Janice.	8/24/2015
Jeff	Create re-order points for the top "50" parts that will be both in the system and physically located in the parts' crib.	8/27/2015
Mary	Create strategy for default locations. Start with Welding.	9/30/2015
Tom	Consolidate part location—after the physical inventory.	1/1/2016

Figure 20 Example Action List

The principles of SATA hold the key for follow-through. Without the strong, consistent sponsorship from the Sustaining Sponsors, above those with actions, follow-up will be hit-and-miss at best.

Beyond that, here are a few basics. Create an action list as shown above. Then, once you accumulate any actions of significance, there are three types of follow-through: formal, ongoing, and long term. *To be successful, a comprehensive strategy incorporating all forms of follow-through must be utilized.* (See the chart on the first page of this chapter.)

Formal Follow-Up: If you had a special meeting to solve a problem, conduct two formal follow-up meetings, minimum, like the ones outlined below. If you already have a weekly or bi-weekly intact work team meeting, start each meeting by reviewing and working the commitments made during the previous week.

For the first situation referenced in the last paragraph, base the number of formal follow-up meetings on the severity, duration, and intensity of the problem. If very severe, the follow-up occurs weekly for a several weeks; if mild, then less frequently.

Process for the follow-up meetings:

- Go through the list of agreements and rate each, asking "Are the commitments being followed?" and "Are you getting the intended results?" Make adjustments or changes accordingly.
- Ask if any other issues have surfaced and set up new agreements if needed.
- Schedule future follow-up meetings, as needed, and adjust the next meeting agenda to ensure effective implementation.

Ongoing Follow-Up: Pay attention, day-to-day, whether commitments made during the meeting are being honored, and make sure that those who committed to actions are making progress. Waiting to check in until formal follow-up will not do.

Long-Term Follow-Up: From time to time, meet to check what is or is not working and, based on that conversation, what could happen differently to ensure success. Since workplaces often change, immediate success does not ensure long-term success. If, in addition, you put in place a quick solution to solve an immediate problem, make sure you revisit it later and make minor tweaks. Sometimes stop-gap solutions which end short-term bleeding hurt productivity in the long run because they have not been revisited.

A note about follow-up—If you put in place a good process but skimp on the follow-up, do not blame the employee or the process for failing. The real problem is the commitment to success and the lack of follow-up. Effective sponsors continue to follow up until the original problem is solved and the organization is functioning more efficiently.

There are many components needed for effective follow-up. The following list illustrates those components. The list is by no means definitive, yet covers the basics. Choose the components needed in your organization, gain strong sponsorship commitment, then make minor tweaks until they work well. Do this and you will create a higher functioning workplace.

Components of Effective Follow-Up

Structured meetings
- Clear Agenda—including how to get topics on it
- Clear time slots for topics
- Right people at right time
- SPA driving meeting and agenda
- Rescheduling of emerging issues, utilize a clear process which allows for appropriate time and involves the right people
- See the Action Item for Factor 10: "Improve Meetings" in *Walking the Empowerment Tightrope*, page 42

Informal check-ins
- Hourly, daily, or weekly

Clear help chain
- Whom and how to call when problems emerge
- Service-level agreements and expectations about response times

Clarity of roles
- Per employee
- Also, for those with whom the above must interact

Allotted time to follow up
Ability to recognize and effectively manage conflicts
- Utilizing key conflict resolution components: clarity, plan, follow-up (Appendix L of *CCIO*)

Ability to recognize and manage systemic issues
- Unclear accountability
- Unclear decision making
- Conflicting priorities
- Competing goals

Sponsor Agent Target Advocate
- Decision clarity (for SATA roles and cross-functional issues)

Effective consequence management
- Single Point of Accountability
- Clear expectations that are behavior-specific
- By-whens
- Overt consequences known
- Consistent application of consequences

More Road Blocks

Several weeks later, Jane walked back into Tim's office.

"Hi, Jane!"

"Hi," Jane said. Once again she had that long look.

"What's up?" Tim inquired.

"Well, I had those conversations with the Sustaining Sponsors, and things really seemed to go well. I certainly saw a spike in better work, yet now again it's starting to slip. I was feeling so good, then many of the same things started happening. That is, action items started slipping."

"Hmm," said Tim, with an inquisitive look on his face. "So, what do you do when they are not getting done?"

"Well," replied Jane, "I just make a mental note and ask them again the following week."

"A mental note?" Tim asked.

"Yes, well, a check, and then I ask them again the following week."

"Hmmm. So, what do the Sustaining Sponsors say when you let them know their employees' tasks are slipping?" Tim asked, with a hint of playfulness in his voice.

"Sustaining Sponsors?" said Jane. "But, I already told them once!"

"Hmmm. Jane," continued Tim, "the task of informing the Sustaining Sponsors, readying the Targets, and education of all key players is an ongoing task. Think of it like a marriage. Stop working on it and you will start failing. Part of your strategy has to be to keep the Sustaining Sponsors up to speed and help them reprimand appropriately, both positively or negatively, to ensure their people have the right priorities so they can accomplish this task."

Tim continued, "You see things from your level that Sponsors cannot possibly see and yet they can manage their people in ways that you cannot possibly manage. *Your task is to help make sure the Sponsors are driving and aligning the Targets when and how they need to, in order for the project to succeed.* That includes helping them praise their people when their employees do excellent work. How often do you meet with them?"

"Meet?" said a surprised Jane. "Well, I haven't after I talked to them a month ago."

"Hmmm. That may or may not be an issue. You have to work through how often to meet with the Sponsors and perhaps its very rarely," said Tim. "Yet, regardless, you need to keep them informed. One highly successful project manager posted a list, showing the action items that are due the next two weeks, on each Sustaining Sponsor's computer. In this day and age, you could do that electronically quite easily. Yet, how you do it has to make sense, based on your current understanding of the project and what is happening in the now."

"The now?" said Jane.

"Yes," answered Tim. "Your particular situation at this moment with your unique project. All managers have priorities and they will keep giving out work and unless they understand the needs of your project they will likely conflict.

Most projects move at different speeds in each department during the different phases of its life cycle. So, figuring out when to inform which Sponsors, about which items, is very situational. That is in part the art of project management.

Yet, many fail at informing Sustaining Sponsors. One common result of this is that managers, i.e. Sustaining Sponsors, who are responsible to deliver on critical parts of projects, get blindsided by suddenly being asked to do something, without enough time to prepare.

In fact, by informing and keeping the Sustaining Sponsors up-to-speed, you may overturn priority conflicts that are, at heart, systemic."

"Systemic?" said Jane with a curious look.

"Yes," said Tim. "If you want something from somebody and their boss wants something else, something has got to give. Certainly, if they try to do them both one of them will not get accomplished. Priority conflicts within organizations are often systemic problems. That does not mean you cannot solve them at the lowest level, yet often you cannot. There must be a way for the business to make decisions based on what is best for its needs. So, if you do not think the Sustaining Sponsors are setting appropriate priorities, you have to raise it to the next level to help get the system aligned. That is an example of generative power, as it helps ensure connection and clarity. By doing so, you may actually find out it is you who is out of alignment. In which case, you would need to adjust accordingly."

"Are you saying I should try to get people in trouble?" asked Jane obviously concerned.

"Not at all," replied Tim. "But I am glad you said that because it is a common misconception. This is not about punishment; it is about alignment and the generative use of power. The question should be: What is best for your organization to be successful in the marketplace? *Alignment is an ongoing task and requires people talking to each other. Generative power always encourages these conversations.* Part of your job is to help those conversations happen as you find them. If you leave the decision up to employees about what the top priority is, they will do their best and choose something that may or may not be right. Or, worse, they fight about what is more important and think the argument's origin is interpersonal when it is not."

"Your organization is large. Does it have a governing body dedicated to this project?" asked Tim.

"Well, yes," said Jane. "I give them updates once a month and Joe, the CEO, sits on it with various other high-level people."

"Perfect," said Tim. "Of course, you need to first clear this with Joe, but I would bring appropriate priority conflicts to that body. In this way, they can help decide what is most important for the business."

"Wow," said Jane. "Now that would add some life into that meeting."

"Yes!" Tim continued. "Use the meeting to help the organization keep looking at itself and what it is doing in terms of aligning to the priorities needed to be successful."

"Yet, Jane," continued Tim, "*do not confuse the governing body for Sponsorship.* They represent sponsorship at a high level but may or may not be over the areas that need to get tasks done. *The task of the Change Agent—in other words any project manager—is to help build and sustain sponsorship at the Sustaining Sponsor level.* Do you remember who that is from Chapter 3?"

"Um, er, not really," said Jane.

"No problem, Jane. Many forget, yet often, ironically, they are actually having battles with the very Sustaining Sponsors with whom they need to be aligning to the work. To remind you: *the Sustaining Sponsor is, by definition, the boss directly above anybody with whom you are working.*

For example, if Shari has a task, her boss is the Sustaining Sponsor of the work. It is *where* work is taking place that is critical here."

"My boss is not the Sponsor?" asked Jane.

"No, replied Tim. "That is where the confusion comes in. Your boss sets your standards and guidelines and is who you are accountable to, yet is *not* the Sponsor of the work. So, you are in the best place to see the imbalances and raise them up, one appropriate conversation at a time."

"Wow," Jane says, with a calm knowing but an obvious excitement that comes from clarity of task and meaning. "You are really just teaching me to use who I am, to push the business, in ways they perhaps have not had the courage to do before. I think I am both scared and exhilarated!"

"Excellent!" Tim said. "You are right on! Your task as a Change Agent is to help push the system, appropriately, in the direction of alignment. Say nothing when tasks slip and you are doing what I call *under-functioning*; pretend you are people's bosses and you are doing what I call *over-functioning* (see Chapter 11).

Both of those concepts involve de-generative use of power by either demeaning people or avoiding obvious alignment conversations. I am asking you to be aware when you slip, because we all do, and to use your personal authority and knowledge of generative power (see p. 71) to encourage the difficult conversations that will get the business aligned and working in the same direction."

"Under what?" said Jane. "That sort of sounds like what I do. I mean I want people to like me and all, yet I want to learn how to be a bit tougher. Of course, I suppose sometimes I can also be a bit pushy!"

"Here," Tim said with a smile, "let me go to my favorite board and talk about some common SATA mistakes . . .

◊◊◊

Read Chapter Eleven

CHAPTER 11

Common Mistakes in Utilizing SATA

Plant Manager: "OK, for a change this large we must appoint good Sponsors!"

Consultant: "No, Joe, you don't appoint Sponsors; they already exist. You identify them and create a plan to get them in alignment!"

Plant Manager: "Wow, I have been missing that point. No wonder some of those major changes have failed! I have been asking my project managers to over-function, and worse yet, getting upset at the resisters. OK, let's chart this and build a plan to get our system into alignment!"

The above conversation represents a common error in how organizations think about work and change: confusion about how authority works in their systems and lack of knowledge of SATA.

The next mistake is seeing SATA as a thing to do once, versus as an ongoing reality in every scenario. Once you stop working on getting your organization aligned and building sponsorship for the work that needs to get done, then you will begin to fail in some areas.

There are many ways by which projects, daily work, and large initiatives fail. The good news is that you can avoid these failings by understanding how to apply SATA correctly.

What follows is a conversation about some of the most common ways SATA gets out of whack in organizations. This basic understanding will help you to lead your organization by thinking through ways to ensure alignment and effective work. Ironically, most of the following scenarios get solved by the right interactions between the right people. Organization alignment happens one conversation at a time.

Project Chart ≠ Map of Legitimate Authority

The rule is: if the project manager of a team also does their performance evaluations, that manager, by definition, is their sponsor. Most of the time, however, the project team consists of members who report to bosses other than its project manager. In fact, often in large organizations there are multiple concurrent projects running with some key members on more than one. Therefore, they must work with many project managers at the same time. If that is the case, then the dynamics of SATA *must* be understood or workplace misalignment is *likely*.

The following chart represents a typical project team.

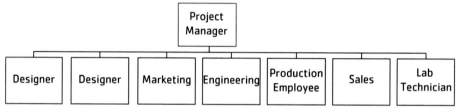

Figure 21 Scenario 4 Project Team with Direct Reports

If the project manager needs the production employee to do a task that is on the critical path of the project, and he or she actually does their performance reviews, then the chart below represents the SATA map.

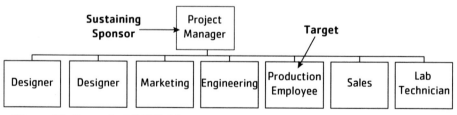

Figure 22 Scenario 4 SATA Map

The problem, of course, is that it is rare for the project manager to have sponsor authority over project team members. In reality, project creation nests inside a pre-existing organization structure. Most likely, the project team resembles the following chart:

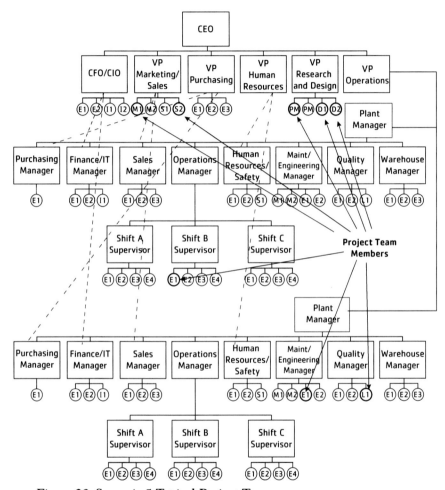

Figure 23 Scenario 5 Typical Project Team

Please note that on the previous chart the project manager has no direct reports; therefore, he/she does not Sponsor anyone, by definition. Most organizations miss or are confused by this critical fact. The job of the project manager and, indeed, the Initiating Sponsor is to learn how to build sponsorship for all team members so they are cleared to perform the tasks necessary in order for the project to succeed.

Given this, let us return to the scenario where the project manager needs a production employee on his project to complete a task critical for

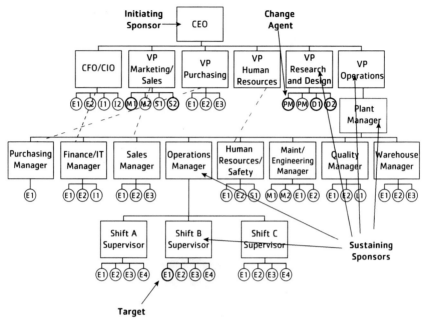

Figure 24 Scenario 5 SATA Map

the project to meet its timeline. Once again, who is the Sponsor of the work? Figure 24 above shows the SATA map.

In this case, the Sponsor of the work is Shift leader B. Does that surprise you? The PM, or Project Manager, is a Change Agent as well. All project managers are Change Agents since they have no legitimate authority over the people they are leading. Of course, they have other forms of power, but the ability to write their performance review is normally not one of them. A project manager must perform a distinct list of duties in order to help the system function appropriately. (See Appendix B for this list in the form of an assessment.)

Project managers face a major task: how to use their position to align and educate the organization. If done well, they can then efficiently work through critical issues and problems associated with implementation success. Awareness of SATA facilitates this clarity. In contrast, if you treat your assigned project team as if you have legitimate authority over them when you do not, your project will likely suffer. Competing priority issues may arise when their "real" boss hands them assignments that potentially impact your project timeline. Instead, be aware of SATA dynamics and create a structure to resolve priority issues between project work and day-to-day assignments.

Project managers, aware of their leveraging role in the system, bring the right players together during key moments of conflict. Thus, they more quickly resolve issues and keep the project on track.

Thinking SATA is a Top-Down Theory

Lead team member to their boss the Plant Manager: "I want you to make sure that if an executive team member talks to me about anything, that they have cleared it with you first!"

Plant Manager: (appropriate response) "Hey, wait a minute, I will work to stay aligned with the executive lead team, but I need you to raise the issue if you think you cannot a) do what they want and b) think they are asking you to do something outside of the priorities that I have given you. But I cannot guarantee each time they talk to you that they will have talked to me first, nor would I want that."

A common mistake when people first hear of SATA is to think it's about following a chain of command and doing things top-down only. That is far from the truth in effective organizations. *In an effective organization, all employees should be able to talk to any other employee, no matter which department.*

Of course, if you are starting a major new project or initiative, you should first build commitment and alignment before you start trying to inform or take up a significant portion of an employee's time. However, to get small things accomplished, it is completely dysfunctional to always use the chain of command.

Effective Targets help ensure system alignment by understanding the boundaries of time they could be pulled from their primary job. If a Sponsor, Change Agent, or Advocate starts asking for time and it appears it will disrupt their clear priorities, then it is their job to get the system back in alignment by directing them to their Sponsor to have real conversation about priorities.

No matter your role, be it Sponsor, Change Agent, or Target, it is your job to constantly clarify your priorities and tasks. Victim behavior is subtle and it amounts to blaming the other. It is easy to slip into when there is a lack of clarity of priorities, roles, or tasks. If you, a Target, have a boss (Sponsor) who needs to work on personal authority (pp. 75 & 218), or vice versa, then the risk of victim behavior increases. The solution is to stay calm and talk about the unclear situation in a non-blaming way.

The rule is: if you find that priorities are starting to compete, *solve them at the lowest level possible.* If it cannot be solved with the person or persons involved, then get the right Sponsor(s) involved to reset the priorities. One of seven deadly wastes to a lean manufacturing person is movement. Movement means extra steps. The next chart illustrates this through use of a spaghetti-type chart, a common method used in the lean manufacturing world.

In this scenario, warehouse personnel E1 wants some help with something on the floor. So, he enlists the Chain of Command to get it done.

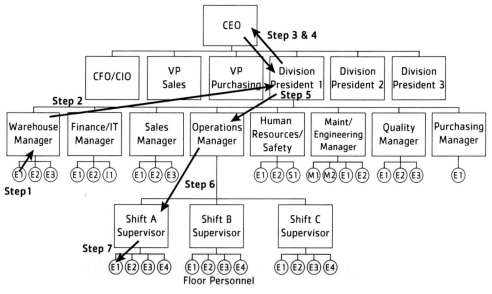

Figure 25 Top-down SATA Confusion 1

In the top-down model above, it takes seven steps to get permission to do the task on the floor. It involves six, maybe seven, people as well. This type of managing creates confusion and greater possibilities for delay or miscommunication. Think of the old communication game called "telephone" and it is not hard to see how there could be problems. Albeit, most will read this and say my example is skewed, but I wanted to include it because it represents the extreme literal example of top-down thinking.

On the following page is a more typical dysfunctional style. In this scenario, again it is warehouse personnel E1 who wants some help with something on the floor. So, he/she enlists the Chain of Command to get it done.

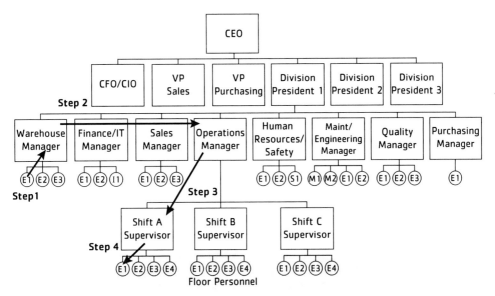

Figure 26 Top-down SATA Confusion 2

Even in the example above, it takes four steps to get permission to do the task on the floor. It involves four or five people. It is easy to see the waste in both of the prior scenarios. The top-down rules were likely put in place as over-compensation for not having managed the employees properly, and for realizing that some employee activities were not add-ing perceived value. When rigid rules get put in place, it can be a quick fix to solve obvious dysfunction. In the long run, however, productivity can and will suffer. So please, if you need a quick fix, do so, but do not keep it in place indefinitely. Instead, circle back and slowly create a more functional work place. In this case, it would be where employees can talk to one another and, yet, know how to push back when requests will hurt their work being accomplished or will fall outside of the clear directions given by their boss (Sponsor).

In contrast to the first few scenarios, the next chart shows a more functional pattern but with clarity of sponsorship. In this case, warehouse personnel E1 who wants some help with something on the floor. So, he/ she talks directly to floor personnel E1.

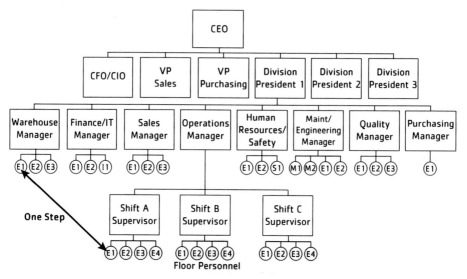

Figure 27 Top-down SATA Confusion 3

OK, you may think this is silly to point out, but people often tell me that they won't go and talk to so-and-so unless it is cleared. Also, I have heard bosses say: "You cannot talk to my people unless you talk to me." My hope is that there are healthy boundaries put in place that don't allow a complete free-for-all, but stop the system from being so rigid that it creates another type of dysfunction. All managers are responsible to keep their people task-focused; however, the goal is a dynamic and flexible system with clear boundaries and expectations.

Top-down thinking in its worst form creates control issues, unnecessary boundaries, and lack of trust. Sign-offs are another form of this. The principle of sign-offs is the same principle that creates new attendance policies when a few people abuse the old one. I want people to manage their employees and hold them accountable. If a few abuse a policy, there is no need to craft a new, seemingly more perfect process to solve the issue. Don't get me wrong; at times there are legitimate reasons to create new policies, but often new policies are put in place as a result of managers who do not know how to utilize their personal authority (p. 75) to apply appropriate consequence management. In other words, if there are already policies in place, use them effectively to manage your employees.

Often sign-offs and approvals for contracts are examples where counter- measures to abuses can bog down your system. A counter- measure is a lean manufacturing term that means creating a process to work around something that is creating a problem in the system. Problems occur when you do not hold people accountable who abuse policies or rules. Ironically, the solution most or many organizations put in place is to create too many controls which hurt everyone. *Processes don't hold people accountable; people do.* Even if you have the perfect process, you still have to do your job as a manager and hold those who break the rules accountable.

Over-Functioning

Essentially, the most traditional way to talk about over-functioning, related to SATA, is when you, without having authority, tell others that they have to do what you say. ***In other words, it is acting as if you are boss when you really aren't.*** Over-functioning happens most when you are in a Change Agent role and you cannot get what you need from the Target.

Although it can be called micro-managing, another form of this pattern may occur for those in the role of Sponsor (see p. 111 "Boundary issues related to but not the same as SATA"). In this form, the boss gets too involved in ways that stop the work or thinking of others. Handing down solutions, instead of handing down problems to solve, is one form of this.

The boss who not only tells people what to do but also exactly how to do each step of the solution is the boss who is over-functioning in role.

Of course, once in a while you may have to do this, especially while giving direction to new employees, but it becomes a problem if you are continually doing it and working harder than your employees. Instead, lead by setting clear expectations and goals, gaining clarity of task components, clarifying problems and who is to work on solving them, holding people accountable, deciding resource needs, and remaining diligent around follow-up to ensure success. Most Sponsors need to work more at directing and leading and less at over-functioning and getting heavily involved with tasks that their employees can do and, most often, understand better than they.

The most common form of over-functioning occurs in the role of the Change Agent. In most organizations over-functioning continually happens and creates all sorts of unnecessary problems. A typical example in the manufacturing world is the tension between maintenance, quality, scheduling, and the floor. Scenarios such as floor personnel not being ready for the scheduled preventative maintenance on a machine, or not wanting to scrap product that a quality person on the previous shift had accepted, often results in finger-pointing at people or departments, versus raising and addressing the organization's misalignment. That individual focus breeds over-functioning. The solutions could involve individual components but a systemic focus is what is most often missed.

The following diagram describes over-functioning in its simplest form.

This scenario entails a Maintenance Mechanic who wants to complete work on the floor, but in order to do so, needs the help of Shift Worker 1. Upon arrival, he finds out that Shift Worker 1 is not ready or willing to do the work:

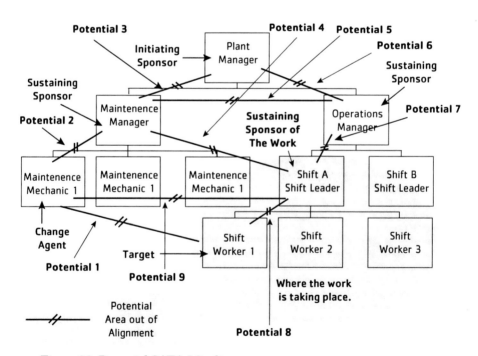

Figure 28 Potential SATA Misalignment

The chart on the previous page identifies the potential area(s) out of alignment. Each of these could contribute to tension between the two employees involved and increase the odds of over-functioning. As you can see, even in just one task on the floor I have highlighted <u>nine</u> potential areas where misalignment could occur.

Here is how the scenario sometimes plays out in a system that is out of alignment:

> If Maintenance Mechanic 1 (MM1) goes to the floor to do preventive maintenance on the machine and the Shift Worker 1 (SW1) is not ready, then MM1 gets upset and blames it on the employee. MM1 then goes back to his department and shares it as yet another example of how screwed up the floor is.

Here is how it could work if you are aware of systemic dynamics:

> If MM1 arrives ready to do preventive maintenance on a machine and SW1 is not ready, they simply re-negotiate for when SW1 is ready so MM1 can return then to complete the work. *Remember, always solve SATA issues at the lowest level.* If it becomes a pattern and the floor is never ready, then the maintenance employee recognizes that something beyond the floor personnel and him is going on. MM1, blaming no one, assumes system misalignment, and says, "There must be some mistake. I thought we had clear times for these PMs. Obviously, that is not the case. I will talk with our bosses to clear this up, and put in place a better system to get this on-going task done."

Since the system is out of alignment, the people who can solve it are most likely the ones who are highlighted above, represented by the potential areas out of alignment: 1, 2, 4, 5, 8, and 9. The systemic view is that the conflict or misalignment is happening not between the floor personnel and the maintenance worker (Potential 1), but it could be out in a whole number of places that I have highlighted above. It may be as simple as the maintenance manager or shift leader forgetting to tell their employees about a change of schedule, or as difficult as the system being out of alignment all the way up the chain of management. Perhaps the confusion is between the shift leader and the maintenance manager, or possibly the operations manager, or even scheduling could be involved.

Clearly there is an alignment issue that needs solving, and clearly there are many areas that could be out of alignment. If you do not solve system issues, what appear to be interpersonal issues will happen throughout your workplace.

The chart on page 168 shows all the potential areas out of alignment, but remember, solve it at the lowest level and only move up the chain if the system remains stuck. In this case, potential 1, 2, 4, 5, 8, and 9 are the most likely places to start.

Over-functioning, like under-functioning, or black holes, are systemic issues that can be solved with remarkable ease if you are aware and are willing to use appropriate backbone. If you are unaware, you may just blame the employee for raising the issue or think that he lacks gumption.

Under-Functioning

Under-functioning is another common mistake in relation to how SATA works within all organizations. It can be summed up by the word "avoidance." It is not just in tasks, but in raising awareness to critical issues that need to be managed well in order for the organization to be successful. *Therefore,* **under-functioning** *is letting tasks, projects, or timelines slip by without doing enough to help the system decide if they are important enough to give proper time and resources to them.* Another form of it is avoiding managing a person or situation due to whatever reason you may have. The manager who gives orders but never follows up to ensure they are completed is also under-functioning. The employee who lets critical meetings or tasks slide without raising their importance to the Sustaining Sponsor, who needs to give them proper priority, also is under-functioning. Allowing a failure by doing nothing to raise systemic awareness is, by definition, under-functioning.

In relation to SATA, under-functioning is a relatively new concept. During my years of internal and external consulting, I began to notice this pattern in organizations beyond what is traditionally taught. Over-functioning helps explain some aspects of how systems get stuck with unclear and confused authority, yet it misses other aspects.

Many people allow things to slip by or go unnoticed. These employees are acting under the real authority they are expected to exercise (whether clarified or not). Not stepping up and taking appropriate authority adds a critical piece as to why tasks do not get done, project timelines start missing deadlines, and change efforts fail.

Here are some examples of how under-functioning has impacted some fairly common work situations:

- A Change Agent in the role of project manager canceled a scheduled follow-up meeting (without consultation with the boss of those in the meeting) because "he didn't want to bother people" despite the fact that the project was worth millions and the boss wanted it to happen.
- A Sponsor did not want to have his longtime employee be the project manager for a multi-million dollar project. Instead, he had three people co-lead the project to avoid "hurting feelings." Of course, having three people co-leading is dysfunctional; it increases the odds of battles over direction.
- A Target/Advocate did not raise a problem with his supervisor because "he did not want to bother the boss," even though the issue was critical to getting production back up and running.

Under-functioning happens more often in organizations than over-functioning. It results in work not getting done, projects slipping, deadlines being missed, and potentially huge financial loses. Based on this belief, I consider under-functioning as a standard part of SATA. Moreover, under-functioning also helps explain behavior for all SATA roles.

Here are some common ways under-functioning shows up for each role:

Sponsors: Feather Ruffling Avoidance

Whenever an employee needs to have a tough conversation—or clear authority is not put in place—but it does not happen out of the fear of upsetting someone. It results in compromises in completion of work, decisions, or slipped timelines.

Change Agents: Letting Timelines, Meetings, and Tasks Slip

Anytime a task, timeline, or meeting is allowed to slide without conscious choice by the Sustaining Sponsor who must make sure that work is balanced between the short- and long-term functioning of the business.

Advocates/Targets/Change Agents: Holding Issues

Whenever an employee is aware of a critical issue, yet does not tell the sponsor; it remains unresolved. The likely result is work not being completed or quality being compromised.

Any SATA Role: Conflict Avoidance

Anytime more than one person or group has differences with each other that, if left unresolved, will likely mean work will not get completed on time and with quality.

Of course, this is not an exact science. The key question here is: "Does the business potentially suffer because of this behavior?" And, yes, there are other systemic, individual, and interpersonal issues at play that help create the dynamics above. Humans often have a hard time with conflict, including listening and receiving difficult information. There is a tendency to want to tread lightly on others' emotions, which is appropriate at times, but detrimental at others. All these and more help increase under-functioning in businesses.

Since it clearly happens in most organizations, the question becomes: "What can be done about it?" The answers to this question are many, and they range from total culture change to one-on-one coaching. Using SATA as a model is a good starting place to set clear expectations for all SATA roles through dialogue with the Sustaining Sponsor(s) and all key players about what to do if the aforementioned behaviors arise. In Chapter 6, I give guidelines for how to use SATA to analyze any situation.

Interplay between Over- and Under-Functioning

There is interplay between over- and under-functioning at play in most situations. If you are trying to get work done in another area and you keep pushing when the people are not able to deliver, by definition you are over-functioning. To solve that problem, you must involve the right people in the system in order for it to have a chance of becoming aligned (see Figure 28 on p. 168).

Failure to do so and continual pushing paradoxically means that you are under-functioning in your role to keep the system healthy. All roles in SATA have a responsibility to keep the system aligned so the workplace maintains functionality. The goal is system alignment and there is always a fine line to tread when working outside of your area. Being flexible if things are not happening is good to a certain degree, but letting it slide too long is under-functioning. In contrast, pushing so hard that you create conflict, tension, and perhaps even misguided blame is over-functioning with the employee, yet under-functioning in system alignment.

The Black Hole of Sponsorship

Black holes happen when the Initiating Sponsor or some other high-level Sustaining Sponsor decides to create a change and pushes it too fast before the whole system can get aligned to support it. By doing this, they skip the conversations and clarity needed to make sure a) it is really the right thing for the organization; b) it is solving critical issues that at least some in the organization believe will help get better business results; c) the organization has the proper support in terms of time and resources for it to be successful; and finally, d) there is enough visibility and clarity through system alignment that the Sustaining Sponsors will not inadvertently undermine the initiative or change.

Black holes are about impatience and quick fixes. They skip the work needed to align the organization. Without those conversations to ensure that the Sustaining Sponsors between the top and where the change will take place are clear and aligned, there is a great chance that neither enough resources nor time will be forthcoming for it to succeed. I do not believe this dynamic is intentional; I think it is a result of there being a finite amount of time combined with pressure to make things happen. With limited resources in all organizations, the work to create alignment is critical in order to stay focused. Black holes represent moments where organizations forget that fact.

The following chart represents the black hole.

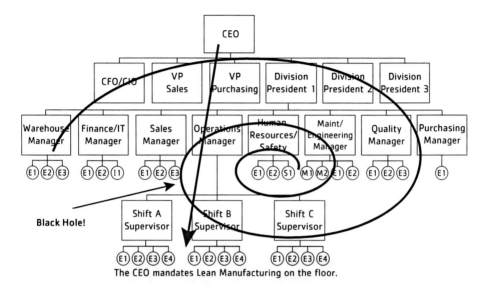

Figure 29 The Black Hole of Sponsorship

"Black holes" are a major reason why so many initiatives and major changes fail. Without real alignment to an initiative, change, or project, the likelihood that the organization will maintain the persistence and focus needed to achieve results is slim. If you live in an organization that rewards people for duking it out to get things done versus spending the time to align the system for change, then you will pay the price. Likely, the result will be departments, initiatives, and projects failing and blame being cast on those very same individuals who were supposed to duke it out, but, ultimately, lose out to dysfunction in the system.

The only way out of a black hole is through real conversations to determine and set priorities and ensure enough resources to complete the task or initiative with quality and on time. That may mean saying yes to some things and, at the same time, saying no to others. There are not many organizations with unlimited resources; there are always numerous good ideas to implement. Alignment can only happen through dialogue by the managers. It needs to happen from the top and throughout the organization down to where the proposed work will take place. Ironically, most think they do not have the time for such conversations. Instead, they settle for wasting millions of dollars in poorly sponsored work. This is a clear pay-now-or-pay-later scenario.

When the Change Comes from the Top

Usually, workplace changes come to the Initiating Sponsor for approval. Examples of such advocacy include new ways to do research and design, purchasing initiatives, department redesigns, new strategies and tactics, changes in policies, etc. There are rare times, however, when a top-level boss brings a practice or initiates a change that is uniquely his or hers. In this case, the CEO or top leader must adhere to a clear set of principles in order to succeed.

The following six points are not necessarily meant as a chronological set of tasks. Rather, they should be seen as a set of guidelines to ensure positive results.

1. **Align your direct reports:** Align your direct reports and hold them accountable for the change. Make sure they fully understand the change with its pluses and minuses. They must hold their direct reports accountable until all affected employees are aligned to support this change.

2. **Align the rest of system:** Initiate and maintain a process to align the groups below yours for the change. This could be accomplished at their weekly meeting or in a large group meeting. One talk will not be enough. You must provide information; let the work groups understand implications, and then follow up, making minor tweaks until the system in aligned. Alignment is an ongoing process, not an event. Stop working on it and it starts falling apart.

3. **Advocate your change:** Beyond your direct reports, recognize and use your strength of advocacy to make sure key managers and employees fully understand what you want to do and why you want to do it. You have positional power in the organization, but most employees tend to pay the most attention to the person who writes their performance assessment. Therefore, you can align and advocate, but beware if you try to hold accountable people who are not your direct reports. Do so by holding *your* direct reports accountable, not

by attempting to hold people accountable over whom you have no direct authority.

4. **Be open to influence:** While you know what you are trying to do, if you impose it the way you did it before, you will miss many in the organization who know the particulars of this business in ways you cannot. Instead, make sure you get the distinction between "adapt" and "adopt," illustrated in *Cultural Change in Organizations,* Appendix I. Then set clear boundaries in what must be adopted, and what can be adapted during the implementation process.

5. **Beware of trying to inspire:** That is, the ability to motivate by giving impassioned speeches is OK as long as it fits into who you are and what you believe. Beware of using inspirational speeches as a primary tactic. Most employees do not want slogans or jargon; they want facts and honesty. Use inspiration if you can, but be careful not to rely on it too much.

6. **Education:** Inform everyone about the facts of the change: how easy or difficult it will be, what the potential pitfalls and benefits are, and how much extra work it will include, especially in the implementation phase. Share successes and drawbacks and keep helping people learn and understand until they have no more questions and are comfortable. Open, two-way communication is a key to successful new practices, but in order for your employees to engage intelligently and have competent interactions, you must first spend time to educate them.

7. **Clear and measurable goals:** This may sound like a duh, but many changes are started without any means to measure whether results are being achieved. Any new process, practice, or change should be tied to the bottom-line results for the business in some critical dimension and should have measurable goals that, once achieved, all can see the direct impact on the bottom line. The goals also must be balanced like "increase sales and reduce returns." If you achieve one goal, but by doing so it creates problems in other areas, then your goals are out of balance. If you achieve your goals and it does not impact the bottom line, then perhaps you are measuring the wrong things, have unbalanced goals, are solving the wrong problems, or the actual change or practice was not the right one for your business.

If you have no way of measuring the change, all you can do is guess whether it is having the impact you want. *If the change is important enough to do, it is important enough to measure.*

Change from the top is tricky yet doable. You have the advantage of being the Initiating Sponsor by default, so getting people's attention is easy. On the other hand, there is also a greater chance of creating a "black hole of sponsorship" (see p. 174). The steps above, if done with diligence, will help avoid this and ensure success. The challenge is to significantly involve those who must change and to stay open to influence. Then with persistence, patience, and drive you will succeed.

Distinction Between the Sponsor and Sponsoring

"The job Harry had didn't work out; you know, the organization didn't get the sponsorship thing."
"I was doing a training and the plant manager walked in. He was a terrible sponsor and wasn't supportive at all."
—countless over-functioning Change Agents

I am sure you have seen this: employees upset because the manager of the people they are working for doesn't support their task. What they are missing, however, is the reality that the boss is either sponsoring the work or is not. The above scenarios could involve over-functioning change agents or advocates who haven't successfully gained sponsorship for their ideas. **Beware if you go forward without proper sponsorship from the boss of the people with whom you are working.** The reality is that Targets always know, even if they support what you want. The distinction between being the Sponsor and Sponsoring is critical and foundational. Since time and resources are limited, all bosses have to choose what they will actively drive or "sponsor." Identifying the Sponsor is the first step. Finding out whether they will Sponsor you—by supporting, condoning, and driving the change you want—is next.

If a Sponsor of the work does not support what you are doing, you may be over-functioning. At least you are under-functioning in your role to help the system get alignment. Once you work to gain alignment, you will find out what the Sponsor does support. If you help them drive that, then they will readily Sponsor the work. Do not make the mistake of thinking that just because you regard it as important a boss will Sponsor it. In that case, you are an Advocate, and you must do the work to build sponsorship.

This chapter is intended to help avoid some common pitfalls associated with SATA. Any change takes commitment and persistence to make sure it is done effectively. By avoiding these traps, your change of success increases.

Analysis Paralysis

Another afternoon session in Tim's office . . .

"Hi, Tim!"

"Hi, Jane! How are you?"

"Great! I really appreciated our last talk because it has helped me to think systemically when I run into problems.

"I was actually hoping that all this knowledge would forever make my life easier, but now I get it that it really just gives me clear ways to help our workplace function better. Yet, what I have found is that when I go into the tension, I come out at a better place. Prior to getting my role in over-functioning, for instance, I just blamed others, got upset, yet the problems of work not getting done seemed to remain more often than I wished.

A few weeks ago, however, I had an interaction that seemed different."

"Different?" Tim said. "Tell me how."

"Well, one of the people with an ongoing task to get my analytics has been a thorn on my side. I went to him again to ask for more info. He said 'No,' and 'It will be a few days.' Instead of pushing him harder, my normal MO, I asked, Why is this so hard? This is clearly what you are supposed to give me weekly?

His reply surprised me. He said, 'Look, Jane, it may seem that way to you, but I have deadlines for my boss and several others who need things from me. By no means are you first on my list.' At first I wanted to start yelling, but then I remembered our talk, and realized that I had no legitimate authority over this guy. Clearly his statement revealed a systems issue. So I said, 'Wow, Joe. Thanks for that. OK. I will meet with your boss to get this cleared up.'

"But, Tim," continued Jane, "I did exactly what you told me to do, yet what came next surprised me. He then said, 'What are trying to do? Get me in trouble?' I was shocked and startled, but unless we had the talk about *system alignment, sponsorship,* and *generative power* I would not have been able to respond with clarity."

"So I said, '*Joe that is not it at all.* But thanks for sharing your concern. *It is the system that is out of sorts. I need to talk to your boss to find out where it is breaking down. Is it my mistake? Or perhaps he and my boss are confused?* I need this data but maybe you should not be getting it for me? To be clear, I just want it to be easy and without the tension we go through. It is obvious to me you have plenty to do.'"

"Wow," said Tim. "What happened next?"

"Well," Jane said, "Joe really calmed down and seemed thankful. Then I talked with his boss and he was not even aware of the task. He then decided to sit down with my boss and iron out exactly what we need and when.

The following week I got the info on time and—the best part— without asking. The person assigned to it sent it without any hassle. I guess I was wrong in a sense: alignment does not ensure all problems go away and seems to take extra time up-front, but over the last few weeks certain tasks that are now aligned are working so well that I can focus on other things, more important things. I am starting to love this stuff more and more."

Tim sat back feeling gratified and happy for his client.

◊◊◊

As quickly as it came, the feeling vanished. Suddenly, Ed burst in the room looking obviously perplexed.

"Ed, how are you? What is happening?" Tim said.

Ed emoted, "Cats! I am herding cats! And I am sooo tired of it!"

"Cats?" Tim replied.

"Well, yes! But I guess Jane already filled you in," replied Ed.

"Well, she was telling me about the data from—" Tim started so say.

"No!" Ed broke in. "Not that! We got that one fixed! I mean the major milestones that keep slipping! Don't they get it or are they OK with the project being late?"

"Hmmm. Sounds like a drag but, to help, I need a little more info. What are you talking about?" asked Tim.

"Tim, we have four or five major decisions to be made in the next few weeks, or we will never make it. They are big and complicated and, so far, I see no real progress," replied Ed.

"Oh, I see." Tim said. "Now I am gaining clarity. Can I ask a few more questions?"

"Yes, please," Ed replied.

"Is it clear who will make the decision?" asked Tim.

"Yes! Of course," replied Ed!

"To a single point of accountability?" Tim continued.

"What? A single point?" Ed blurted with obvious anger. "Tim, these decisions are large and complicated, so everybody has to take part."

"OK," said Tim. "I get that, but just because a lot of people have to be involved does not mean that they all make the call. Unless there is clarity of decision making in these complicated scenarios, likely things will slip. If you have nobody clearly accountable, then you are using *consensus by default.*"

"What?" Ed responded, "By default?"

"Yes, Ed, but first, can I ask one more question before I continue?" Tim inquired.

"Sure. Fire away!" Ed exclaimed.

"Do the decisions run across departments that eventually all report up to Joe?" Tim inquired.

"Well, yes, of course. Almost all departments in our business!" said Ed.

"OK, great!" Tim said. "Ed, remember Joe said anytime we need him, we should call him in? I think he needs to be a part of this conversation. Could you give him a call and see if he is available?"

"Joe? OK, let me call him," Ed replied.

Amazingly a few minutes later, Joe walked in the door looking rather invigorated. He said, "Hi, Tim! How are you?"

"Great, Joe. I must say you are looking rather happy!" Said Tim.

"Thanks, Tim. Yeah, I am beginning to feel better about things. Jane, here, has been doing a great job and it seems we are moving on this thing," Joe responded.

"Hold onto your excitement, Joe. Weze gotz some problems," said Ed.

"Dang! Can't I remain happy for a little while longer?" pleaded Joe with a slight smile.

All of them had a small chuckle before Ed spoke again. "Joe, there are some major decisions that are in risk of putting the project in jeopardy."

"Decisions?" Joe said. "Like what?"

Jane spoke up, "Well, one is finalizing the design. People keep adding things and to do some of them will cost money and resources."

Joe began, "You know, we have always had problems with speed when we make decisions, and sometimes we go around in circles for months, even years, yet delaying the final call benefits us very little, if at all. We have so much talent in this organization. Surely there is a better way?"

"Joe, I am glad you said that, because it is what I was suspecting," said Tim. "Do you mind if we spend some time on authority and decision making?"

"Please!" said Joe, with a learner's spark of enthusiasm in his voice.

At that, Tim got up and began to write on his whiteboard and at the same time he started to speak, "This represents the full range of authority . . . "

◊◊◊

Read Chapter Twelve

CHAPTER 12

Decision Making

Introduction

Consultant: "Mike, we have been talking about this problem for 45 minutes now. How much information do you need in order to make a decision? It seems pretty clear that this is big enough that you should do something."

Manager (surprised and suddenly sitting up in his seat): "Um, yeah, OK, well you're right. I knew enough after ten minutes but just sort of checked out. All right, so this is how I want us to handle it . . . "

One of the most basic tenants of leadership is the ability to make a decision. Yet many leaders are hesitant to decide, for various reasons. ***Leadership is about taking the chance to move towards your desired goals even if some doubt the direction in which you are headed.*** Your objective is to move towards goals previously thought unattainable. Clearly articulate them and then utilize your employees' opinions and knowledge in creating a plan to get there.

Along the way, clarity of decision-making authority is essential: who decides, who has influence, what the parameters are, and when these decisions need to be made to maximum success. Many managers pay these components of decision clarity little or no attention. *Decision making is ultimately about leading with clarity and creating healthy workplaces.*

The scenario above is real. *Just the ability to stand up and make a decision is an act of leadership.* Many are unaware that they are even supposed to do so as leaders of groups. So many let even small decisions wallow out of a lack of awareness, capability, backbone or, most importantly, being held accountable themselves. That's right: if a manager who reports to you is not making decisions, you are the one who needs to hold them accountable to do so. Often, once you break the inertia, there is a fighting chance that the manager will begin to lead. You must, however, be clear about your expectations.

Decision making is key to driving clear structure and accountability in organizations. In Chapter 1, I talk about authority in systems and how to drive clarity of authority in order to create a more functional workplace. Decision making is the key to such clarity. True employee empowerment comes from granting your employees authority to decide specific work scenarios from moment-to-moment.

Employee empowerment is possible and, in fact, easy; yet, ironically, it cannot be obtained by an empowerment program unless it has at its foundation clarity about decision making. Further, that clarity can only happen in each intact work group: the boss and direct reports.

Robert Crosby has studied authority in systems since his early years with disciples of John Dewey and Kurt Lewin. It was not until reading an article in the *Harvard Business Review* entitled "How To Choose a Leadership Pattern," that Crosby began developing his own model of decision making. In this section, I will explore his current model and show how to use it both as a situational model and as a tool to gain clarity of authority throughout the workplace.

Intact Work Groups

As you learned in the section on SATA, a key to understanding sponsorship is the definition of the Sponsor that states: "You can only Sponsor your direct reports." This distinction helps point to the critical importance of the intact work group when clarifying decision making and driving culture change. This is not just my assertion; many foundational thinkers have learned this in the past.

For example, Kurt Lewin's core systems theory from the first half of the twentieth century is B=f(P,E) where B stands for "behavior," f stands for "function of," P stands for "person," and E stands for "environment," points to the importance of the intact work group. His work to improve farming practices in the 1940s when the government failed to implement a program critical to the war effort is a classic example of this. Lewin helped them think through how to get all the people involved for the change to be successful, such as involving farmers' wives and influential peers. When that happened, the change turned into a success.

Carl Whitaker, a prominent family systems thinker, developed his systems theory by working with schizophrenics in a hospital setting. While there, patient improvement was visible. On returning home to the environment that had strongly shaped their behavior, however, almost all had complete relapses. Based on this, he started working only with families when people called about members who were "sick." In fact, he was one of the people who clarified the role of the "identified patient" in the system. In short, what is presented as "*the* problem" is really a symptom of something else happening in the wider system.

Organizations don't have to look far for examples of this. Many send employees to trainings in an attempt to "fix" them. Even those trainings that the employee rates favorably often show little to no change in employee performance upon return. It is my belief that it is the intact work group where lasting systemic change gets created. Do not read this as a bash of training. Certainly much training, especially in the technical realms, is critical to improvement, but to change a culture and to reach greater overall business results, you must focus on the whole system rather than on its parts. Lewin and Whitaker both knew that if you strengthen and clarify all authority structures in the system, then the system itself suddenly and magically starts functioning better.

I have often seen this paralleled in work on aligning goals. When done well, goal alignment gets the managers (parents) all heading in the same direction, each with their own unique goals for their unique departments. Clarifying authority and direction is a basic structure necessary for a healthy system to function. Ironically, with many organizations where I have worked, managers tend to blame incompetence on the production floor for any problems. However, when I spend several days aligning the management team to their goals, suddenly and magically, the production floor starts performing.

Perhaps I have digressed, but the point is *once you focus on the whole system, then change is highly possible.* When you work on clarifying authority and empowering people, you must focus on boss and direct report. Based on this, working with intact work groups is the key to clarity of authority and creating functional workplaces.

Too Autocratic–Too Permissive

At a recent training event, I had participants line up on a continuum about authority in their system from too permissive to too autocratic. I first asked them how relating with authority was a few years ago prior to the sale of their business. A few lined up on the autocratic side, while many lined up on the "too permissive" side. Then I asked them how things were with the current manager: Most clumped towards the middle; the rest stretched towards autocratic.

The current manager was making an effort to lead using the principles in this book. "Explaining their position on the continuum, many mentioned how much structure there is today versus a few years ago," one said "I feel much more pressure today and am held more accountable. Prior to this, I could do what I wanted. Don't get me wrong; I love the workplace today. I am happy we are finally getting somewhere, but I am held accountable more today than in the 15 years I have been here. We have accomplished more in the last few years than we ever have."

This illustrates a point that it is not about comfort necessarily–you must manage this dimension since too much pressure creates problems– rather, it is about leadership and accountability. All people, be it worker or manager, have a comfort level along a continuum of authority from too autocratic to too permissive.

Below is a graph that represents that continuum

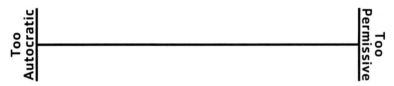

Figure 30 Authority Continuum

It is my belief that this creates issues more ideological in nature than practical. Many have such strong beliefs about authority that they hold their spot on the continuum as the "right" spot to be. The dilemma is that others have a comfort zone at a different spot and, most, also hold their preferred position just as strongly. Many conflicts between boss and employee are due to one preferring too permissive and the other preferring too autocratic. It is also my contention that leadership happens mostly from the middle of this continuum. The next graphic represents my view of leadership in relationship to the authority continuum.

Figure 31 Leadership and the Authority Continuum

Therefore, the boss who is too autocratic must learn to let go and the boss who is too permissive must learn to take charge. The next graph shows that leadership is based on managing from the middle while learning the appropriate strategy for each situation. In fact, all workplaces, like all of life, are situational and, therefore, need flexibility and guidance depending on the situation. Looking back to Chapter 1, delegate as much authority as you can as a leader, but never forget who is ultimately accountable. Do so in a situational way, based on the experience, expertise, and maturity of your employees.

On this basis, Robert Crosby built his theory of decision making.

Robert Crosby's Decision-Making Styles

Robert Crosby had exposure to how groups are influenced by decision-making processes throughout his career. Even in the early T-Group experiences, trainers focused on how decisions were made in groups. It was not until he read Tannenbuam and Schmidt's "How to Choose a Leadership Pattern" in the *Harvard Business Review*, that he developed his own theory of decision making in organizations. What follows is the most recent version informed by our work.

"Decision-Making Style" represents a situational model of leadership. It requires the leader to learn how to utilize four decision-making styles across a continuum while considering factors such as the experience, maturity, and judgment of employees, and the time frame in which to decide. All styles involve employee participation, with the highest coming from the two middle styles.

	Independent	Consultative	Delegation	Group-Oriented	
Too Autocratic	**Decide and tell** Decide by yourself and announce your decision. Dialogue with your employees to make sure that you have been clear.	**Decide after consultation** **Bring Solutions:** Get your employees' input, then decide. **Bring Problems:** Get your employees' solutions, then decide.	**Delegate to an employee** Set clear guidelines, boundaries, and expectations, and create a system of monitoring with your employee(s).	**Delegate to the group** **Majority Vote:** Leader has one vote, gives up veto power. **Consensus:** All agree solution is reasonable after dialogue.	**Too Permissive**

Figure 32 Decision-Making Styles

As I have mentioned previously, leadership comes from managing from the middle, which not only presents a challenge to interpersonal skills but demands a higher level of engagement. All styles are important; however, the ability to be decisive and to make independent decisions at key moments is critical.

Clarity is essential for effective decision making. In order to gain clarity, you must state the decision-making style you are using and then operate from that style. Many, concerned or confused about authority, will skip this type of honesty. Such clarity is the key to creating a culture of accountability and managing from the middle. For example, without clarity of task and a system of monitoring in place, delegation could easily become an exercise in abdication. Without clarity, it is easier to slide into either extreme on the authority continuum.

	Independent	Consultative	Delegation	Group-Oriented	
Too Autocratic	**Decide and tell** Decide by yourself and announce your decision. Dialogue with your employees to make sure that you have been clear.	**Decide after consultation** **Bring Solutions:** Get your employees' input, then decide. **Bring Problems:** Get your employees' solutions, then decide.	**Delegate to an employee** Set clear guidelines, boundaries, and expectations, and create a system of monitoring with your employee(s).	**Delegate to the group** **Majority Vote:** Leader has one vote, gives up veto power. **Consensus:** All agree solution is reasonable after dialogue.	**Too Permissive**

Figure 33 Independent Decision Making

Now let's look at each style a little more closely. The first style, moving from left to right is **"independent decision making."** This style is just as it sounds: leaders decide, then tell their employees the decision.

Of course, a dialogue for clarity is critical for any decision. Independent decisions are the fastest type of decision, as they don't involve immediate dialogue prior to the decision being made. Therefore, safety, goals, and emergency actions in a crisis are made utilizing this style of decision making. Yearly goals are almost always independent decisions, especially in corporate environments, and employee expectations fall under this category as well.

Like all styles, independent decision making is critical for taking action and moving in a desired direction. As a boss, if you are clear about direction, independent decision making is most likely the best way to go. If you are clear about direction but are too permissive in your style, you will not reach your goal.

Additionally, independent decision making must be used to effectively solve work relationship problems between employees and departments. It is your duty as boss to provide structures for working through difficult issues and to ensure that your employees work better together. Many problems in organizations persist because bosses are unwilling or incapable of using their authority (p. 75) to ensure their employees resolve workplace conflicts, and to hold them accountable for the improvements. Ironically, it is this style that must be used if you want your employees to develop any higher-order skills, such as conflict resolution or leadership skills. When employees are left on their own to decide, many will say "I do not need them."

Independent	Consultative	Delegation	Group–Oriented
Decide and tell	**Decide after consultation**	**Delegate to an employee**	**Delegate to the group**
Decide by yourself and announce your decision.	**Bring Solutions:** Get your employees' input, then decide.	Set clear guidelines, boundaries, and expectations, and create a system of monitoring with your employee(s).	**Majority Vote:** Leader has one vote, gives up veto power.
Dialogue with your employees to make sure that you have been clear.	**Bring Problems:** Get your employees' solutions, then decide.		**Consensus:** All agree solution is reasonable after dialogue.

Too Autocratic ← → **Too Permissive**

Figure 34 Consultative Decision Making

The next style of decision making is **"consultative."** In this style there are two options. *Bring a solution* to a problem that you want kicked around to gain input from employees, while making it clear you will have the final say. The next option is to *bring a problem* that you need solved and get help in generating solutions before making the final call. Consultative decision making is a great way to ensure employee input with clear boundaries. Stating at the outset: "I need your input before I make the call" frees employees up to say what they think and to let go of the outcome. This style must be used in fast-moving organizations to ensure you are connected to the needs and conditions of the employees. Mostly consultative decision making is used with your direct reports, but it can, and should, also be used cross-functionally in work between departments, major initiatives, or projects. Ironically, it is also hard to do because it requires communication with people whose views may differ from yours.

Managers who have a hard time listening to dissenting views may either struggle with consultative decision making or cut off half of their inputs, out of intolerance. I suggest giving space for all views while clarifying the decision-making boundaries. Some of those opposing views, after all, may slightly alter and improve the decision or spark actions that may be key for mitigating risk. By doing so, decisions will be made with as much info as possible and fewer blind spots will remain.

To solve major problems and develop solutions that are well conceived and thought-out, consultative decision making is a must. In critical projects we take this beyond the immediate work group and utilize it throughout the organization (see p. 207 for a decision grid). See Chapter 9 to help you think through who should really be involved in various types of organizational decisions.

	Independent	Consultative	Delegation	Group-Oriented	
Too Autocratic	**Decide and tell**	**Decide after consultation**	**Delegate to an employee**	**Delegate to the group**	**Too Permissive**
	Decide by yourself and announce your decision.	**Bring Solutions:** Get your employees' input, then decide.	Set clear guidelines, boundaries, and expectations, and create a system of monitoring with your employee(s).	**Majority Vote:** Leader has one vote, gives up veto power.	
	Dialogue with your employees to make sure that you have been clear.	**Bring Problems:** Get your employees' solutions, then decide.		**Consensus:** All agree solution is reasonable after dialogue.	

Figure 35 Delegation

"**Delegation**" is the third style of decision making; it moves the manager even more towards permissive decision making as it drives authority down the organization to where the work is taking place.

Most employees have situations where they are waiting on a decision from somebody else in order to do their work. All scenarios like that are candidates for delegation. Therefore, by definition, delegation involves moving the responsibility to make specific decision(s), exercised solely by the boss before this, to a subordinate.

While I highly value delegation and suggest using it as much as possible, *I do not suggest suddenly delegating all decision authority in an ideological way.* Instead, be careful and considerate when delegating. Allow the experience and competency of the employee to determine when and how to delegate.

Delegation can and should be seen as an opportunity to train and advance employees in their capabilities and responsibilities. Even employees who are a little uncomfortable expanding their responsibilities could be delegated work as an opportunity for growth. Delegation should be used to help the organization get better results. Make no mistake: *a boss is not absolved of accountability for tasks once they have been delegated.* In fact, it is a common error for a manager to let go of a decision without having developed a system to monitor progress and results. If you do so, you are abdicating, NOT delegating.

There is a series of steps used to delegate effectively. See Appendix E of *Cultural Change in Organizations.* We suggest you use as much delegation as you can, so your organization can move as fast as possible, and decisions are made as close as possible to where the work takes place. Make sure to really delegate versus fall into the trap of abdication.

	Independent	Consultative	Delegation	Group-Oriented	
Too Autocratic	**Decide and tell** Decide by yourself and announce your decision. Dialogue with your employees to make sure that you have been clear.	**Decide after consultation** **Bring Solutions:** Get your employees' input, then decide. **Bring Problems:** Get your employees' solutions, then decide.	**Delegate to an employee** Set clear guidelines, boundaries, and expectations, and create a system of monitoring with your employee(s).	**Delegate to the group** **Majority Vote:** Leader has one vote, gives up veto power. **Consensus:** All agree solution is reasonable after dialogue.	**Too Permissive**

Figure 36 Group-Oriented Decision Making

The last decision-making style is **"group-oriented"** and has two sub-categories, majority vote and consensus. Majority vote usually means garnering 51 percent of the vote to decide. This is not a very practical style in business; it could be used to decide what to have for lunch or something innocuous. It has drawbacks, such as upsetting the 49 percent who voted no.

The other category of group decision making is consensus. I hold to a strict standard of consensus: all who are part of the process have to verbalize consent prior to the decision being made. True consensus takes time and can pander to the most dependent or most vocal. The plus is that if you get a real consensus it can be a better decision at times. Any who have played the game "Lost on the Moon" or "Lost in the Jungle" can easily see the benefits, but there are also drawbacks.

Most who use this style do not hold strictly to it and are unclear they are using it. This increases the likelihood that decisions will get bogged down and take up valuable time. Therefore, it may increase pre-existing hostility in your work culture; employees may be frustrated from a lack of forward movement.

The intention of consensus is inclusion. That intention is golden and a key to solving problems successfully. *Therefore, we suggest that if you use consensus, use a time limit.* We also suggest that you use many strategies to ensure inclusion and engagement of your employees outside of the decision-making style of consensus.

What most don't realize is that all styles of decision making are about participation and inclusion. To truly create a fast-moving organization that empowers your employees and includes the right people in the right areas, you must balance all styles. That balance should be based on the conditions inside of your organization and the maturity and competency of your employees. Of course, that includes the business results you are getting right now. As a leader, utilize some independent decision making, as much of consultative decision making and delegation as possible, and very little of group-oriented.

Only do so, however, by actual need and with a carefully thought-out plan. Based on this, the graphic below represents where leaders should operate along the decision-making continuum.

Figure 37 Leadership and Decision Making

Remember: be practical, and let business results be your guide, If you are getting record results, don't change anything! Unless, of course, your record equates to 65 percent on-time delivery, then you have work to do! The movement to use more consultation and delegation ironically creates a scenario requiring better communication skills. Inclusion and participation of employees is paradoxically about the balance between management authority and employee influence, rather than about trying to put in place an ideology of consensus management.

The Role of Clarity

Clarity is essential for all types of decision making. Even a boss making an independent decision needs to dialogue with their employees about the potential obstacles to success, to gain a deeper understanding of the decisions implications, and to clarify expectations going forward. No decision style works well without interactions to gain clarity. Giving a direction and asking if you are clear is not enough. *After all, if an employee say: "Yes, I am clear," all you know is that they think they are clear.* Clarity comes from dialogue about specific details. Once you get to this place, you can feel more comfortable that execution will be successful.

Your task is to lead with clarity. To do so, decisions and tasks require your interaction until absolute clarity is achieved.

Matrixes

"I have ten bosses."
"I have three bosses."
"Let's see, I have two bosses."
—many employees in most organizations

As large corporations have consolidated over the last 20 years, a trend has been to create a matrix in which one group drives a function over the entire organization. Finance, customer service, inside sales, purchasing, and planning are some of the likely areas. The intention is to save money and to help coordinate multiple locations to keep standards and practices the same. Indeed, at times money is saved and redundancies eliminated. There is also no doubt that centralizing functions like planning, for instance, can help get product shipped to the customer quicker by using the shortest shipping routes, etc.

The downside of this strategy is that it can create confusion and lack of clarity when there are conflicting priorities. This problem is mostly ignored, however, since it is an indirect cost and it involves authority in systems of which some are unaware. The cost of ignoring this downside is poor production, coordination, and execution. The issue is that if you have one or many dotted lines, and a solid line, how do you decide when there is a conflict of priorities? Many organizations decide by the loudest voice or the squeaky wheel.

The solution is remarkable simply, yet difficult to pull off. There must be a conversation with the dotted and solid lines to determine the pinch points in the various scenarios, and a decision process created to resolve each one. Decisions should be made with regard to what is best for the organization, rather than what any one employee thinks or who strong-arms the most. A simple decision grid can be created to solidify this and add clarity (see p. 207 of this book).

The need for businesses to move more quickly will always exist, and every organization has periods of being more or less complex. Create decision clarity in a matrixed environment to ensure that the best possible decisions are made in service to the organization.

Now We Can Move

An hour later, the conversation continued . . .

"You know," said Joe, "Our problem is that people who should make decisions, don't; then people who shouldn't, swoop down several layers to make them. To be fair, it's almost always after days, weeks, or even months of gridlock between departments."

"Which departments?" Asked Tim.

"Just about all," said Joe.

"Hmmm. Well, if that happens, it is a good bet that clarity of decisions across groups is not in place, nor is it properly sponsored. Clarity is not enough. The generative use of power means that the Sponsors at the right levels are using their backbone and personal authority consistently to ensure effective decision making. That means the best people are making the call at the right times to ensure success. I know of no other way to actually move a culture."

"Good luck!" said Ed. "Some people around here will never let go, and most are fearful of them."

"Really? Like who?" said Tim.

"Well, the Director of Product Management for instance, Sally Smith." Ed continued, "No matter what, she does what she wants."

"Doesn't she report to you, Joe?" said Tim.

"Yeah, that is true. But Sally is smart, really smart, and knows so much. She has been here for so long, I really try and stay away."

"Hmmm. Sounds rough," Tim said. "Yet, it also sounds like the lack of clarity is hurting you."

"True," said Ed, "especially during implementation when problems emerge between the Product Manager and the Software Engineers."

"Seriously? Do you have to bring that up? It is so painful," said Jane. "People around here cringe whenever they hear it."

"Yes, and Sally and I don't exactly see eye-to-eye," said Ed.

"Forgive me for asking this, but would someone be willing to fill me in on the pain?" inquired Tim.

Looking at Joe and Ed, Jane hesitated, "Oh wow, OK. Shall I?" On their nods Jane was off. "Tim, it comes down to two words, and it happens during implementations. Is it a *defect* or an *enhancement?*"

"What?" said Tim.

"Well," Jane continued, "to understand this you must realize that we have separate groups that do separate things. Product Managers write the requirements and the Software engineers use those requirements to write the code and produce the software. The better the requirements, the easier it is to make the proper software for the customer. As you may remember, I was hired to be a Product Manager; that means I write requirements and hand them to developers. Of course, now I am in an expanded role as project manager."

"Right, congrats again!" said Tim with a smile.

Joe chimed in, "Tim, sometimes this gets tricky, depending on how good each person is at their role. We have been getting better, but a few years ago we had many new hires writing the software that came from the start-up world. In start-ups, employees do everything. In other words, they write requirements and code. That is cool and exciting, yet it still comes down to sales. No earnings and the start-up fails. We hire a lot of people that are used to the boundaries associated with the start-up world. But here, in a company this large, we create a clear separation between product managers and software engineers.

As you might imagine, this creates beliefs in people that they know both how code should be written, from the product manager side, as well as what the customer really needs, from the software engineer side."

"Yes, I can see how that would create fuzzy ownership at times, especially if your system has had a tendency towards permissiveness," said Tim.

"There you go again, reminding me of that authority thing," Joe said with a smile. "Good point, Tim. It has contributed to it, or at least I imagine it has."

"OK, that seems clear enough," said Tim. "What happens next?"

"Then comes the implementation at the client site. That is really where the fun begins." Jane continues, "As far as I can see, we are no different than many places. But, Ed and Joe, help me out if you see it differently."

"Here is what happens. We start to implement and uncover that the software does not work right. Tim, it could be that the end user at the customer site finds this or someone on our implementation team. Regardless, the software is not working right. The question is: Did the product managers fail at building their requirements or did the software engineers fail at building the software? The answer to that question determines where the ownership lies. If the product managers fail it's an *enhancement* request and if the software engineers fail it's a *defect*."

"And we fight back and forth all the time because it is about cost and who pays," Ed commented.

"Yup," Jane says.

"Painful," adds Joe, cringing.

"Yes, and the fighting can get ugly if the reality is that a major fix is needed. Small fixes are not a problem but if the defect or enhancement means a major rewrite of code, then the pain increases," Jane added.

Joe remarked, "Tim, if this is an enhancement we can push along some costs to the customer and that always makes my financial team happy."

"Yes," said Jane, "and you can imagine what the customer thinks of that."

"How do you clear these things up?" asked Tim. "Since this clearly seems to be a cross-group issue and, with money involved, I bet it can get ugly."

"I'll take this," Ed declared. "Well, Tim, we look at the requirements and ask: Would a reasonable person seeing this requirement assume this is the intent of the law? That is, the intent of the requirements?"

"Ed, who decides?" Tim asked.

"Well, usually we have a meeting with both groups in the room and hash it out," Ed replied.

"You mean the product managers and software engineers fight it out?" Tim asked.

"Yes, and sometimes the decision gets raised all the way up to Sally and me. In fact, sometimes Sally and I end up in a meeting room somewhere arguing about it until we can decide," continued Ed. "And I don't have to tell you but she is tough. I really have to up my game then."

"What is happening to the customer during all this?" Tim inquired.

"Good question," Joe stated. "They wait for us to resolve things and, once in a while, our internal fighting does not get resolved, so we try to push the problem back to the customer. I have, on occasion, taken calls from very angry, important customers after our product managers went back to them saying, 'Oh, this is how we designed it based on the requirements you gave us.'"

"Tim," Jane spoke out, "if it's determined to be an enhancement it takes longer to fix and you can get away with that easier in the customers' eyes. That is, it looks like extra technical work, so it makes sense that it should take longer. For defects, the fixes happen rapidly."

"And, in reality," said Ed, "we have two scenarios right now where this is happening. But, Tim, we have had this struggle forever, so it will always come back to us."

"Yes, and my project is breaking new ground," Jane affirmed. "So, I fear that if we cannot work through these better, we risk wasting months in fighting while we hash out difficult SMART project issues."

"To be clear," said Joe, "even the best product managers have a hard time being perfect at figuring out all of the customer's needs, and writing code and building a software program is not the easiest task. So these fights will likely happen forever."

"So," Tim said, "is it safe to say that your internal process to decide, or lack there of it, negatively impacts the customer?"

"YES!" Another moment of unison occurs.

"Then, I have good news," continued Tim. "You can and will fix this *if* you have the determination."

"Great!" came the response from the group.

"However," Tim continued, "it will take backbone and solving some authority issues to do it and, of course, generative power."

The room got a little somber and Joe spoke, "Why did I not see this coming? OK, tell me more."

"Btw," Tim continued, "it also takes backbone to increase employee engagement. Similar principles are involved with both issues."

"Hmmm," said Joe. "We have been telling employees they are empowered for years and it's been hard for us to get any real change."

"Yes," said Tim. "Since *increasing empowerment is about pushing down and clarifying decision authority,* then it can be truly empowering, *the same is needed to solve some of your cross-functional work issues.* OK, let me go deeper with decision making and include some cross-functional dimensions . . . "

And with that, Tim went back to his favorite board.

◊◊◊

Read Chapter Thirteen

CHAPTER 13

Employee Empowerment

Businesses have squandered millions on so-called "empowerment programs" and "self-directed teams." The problem with most: they fail to understand how authority works in systems and, therefore, get lost in slogans instead of action. Decision-making authority is a key ingredient of employee empowerment; inclusion and involvement are also critical so that worker knowledge is utilized and the day-to-day problems are raised. Employees doing the work know the current problems, past failed remedies, and the reasons why.

A note about past failures—Just because something failed in the past does not mean to not try it again. If you choose to try it again, however, make sure you understand all the reasons it failed and put in place solutions that address them. A common mistake is to blame past failures on the idea, versus system alignment and implementation effectiveness. Another mistake is to keep trying the same thing in the same way, without any adjustments from what you learned from past failures. Listening to all types of employee knowledge (see p. 139) is the path to creating a learning organization.

Empower your employees by using a systematic method that strategically delegates greater decision-making authority (see Chapter 5 in *Cultural Change in Organizations*: "How to Move Towards Increased Employee Autonomy"). Without such clarity of authority, employee empowerment and so-called self-directed teams are doomed to fail, but not due to the usual reasons leaders give: "resistance" or "lack of cooperation." The reason: in a vacuum without clear roles and accountability, power struggles and confusion develops. There must be clarity of who does what, and who decides what and when, for effective work to get done. That clarity must be driven through the formal reporting relationships in your organization. In short, that is the legitimate map of authority as represented by each intact work group of boss and direct reports.

The Integration of Decision Making and SATA

There are essentially two ways to drive decision authority in your system. First, coach and counsel your direct reports to begin to let go of some of their decision authority and drive it downward to where it is closest to the work. This is a slow process that will take time to get moving in your organization. The key here is to make sure you are paying attention to the chain of command. If you are a high-level boss, and you advocate that employees at lower levels should make more decisions, then you most likely will need to start by pushing some of your own decisions to your direct reports. Then hold them accountable to do likewise, and so on, until authority is pushed to the lowest level. Second, methodically teach decision clarity and drive down decision making systematically, work group by work group.

When doing either process, use SATA as a lens to make sure you align your system along the way. The risk is that you push decision making downward yet forget to involve critical mid-level Sponsors (managers) who will inadvertently overturn decisions and cause potential confusion and/or moral issues. In other words, if you do not pay attention to systemic principles while attempting to empower workers at the lower levels, then you will may create a black hole of sponsorship (see p. 174).

I worked with a boss in a family-owned business. The owner wanted to both reduce his hours and maintain business in order to help him free-up time to pursue other interests. He and his employees charted his business, gained clarity of roles and decision making, and then delegated many decisions to them. He held onto a few critical ones but let many go. This simple intervention resulted in 50 hours being reduced to 20 hours with no loss of business and no extra overhead.

The chart on the previous page represents the current state (i.e., how the business was functioning when I started working with them).

Note that employees identified two areas for which there was no SPA! (See p. 118.) It is no surprise that those areas were in complete disarray. Any business situation without a clear single point of accountability

Independent	Consultative	Delegation	Group	No SPA
Marketing and Sales Purchase Vinyl and Consumables Stocking Inventory Product Lines Management Hours Financial Planning Future Business Structure, Functioning of Business	Hiring and Firing Marketing Sales of Equipment Accounting	Sales Call and Tactics How to Respond to Customer Inquiry Shipping A/C Filing, GL, Admin, General Office		Demo Room Lunch Schedule

Figure 38 Empowerment/Decision Making: Current

belongs in that category. It is common to find many tasks or activities without assigned singlepoint of accountability. Sometimes those tasks stay that way hidden under the guise of "Adults will just do the responsible thing." Of course, adults are human and humans make mistakes. When you have tasks for which many have to do yet no single person is held accountable, then there is a great likelihood that you will increase the amount of tension and unnecessary blame within your organization.

In the next step of the process the leader decides the future state of the business. He chose to do so in consultation with his employees. Once decided, he created an action plan with his employees to get clear on what training, actions, or educational needs they had in order to prepare for their future responsibilities. His time frame was five months. This critical step must be included each time you drive down decision authority.

Independent	Consultative	Delegation	Group
Purchase Vinyl and Consumables Management Hours Financial Planning Consultative by Dec.	Hiring and Firing Marketing Sales of Equipment Accounting Marketing and Sales Stocking Inventory Product Lines Formal Job Description and Org Chart	Demo Room Lunch Schedule Purchasing Sales and Equipment Sales Call and Tactics & Customer Inquiry Shipping A/C Filing, GL, Admin, General Office	Mission Statement Consensus With Time Limits

Figure 39 Empowerment/Decision Making: Future

Figure 39 illustrates the owners desired future state. Note: All of this happened in a group dialogue with all seven employees present; I facilitated. Additionally, the items on chart are either by role or by a Single Point of

Accountability. It is important to remember that groups don't make decisions; people do, so you must clarify who is responsible for making any decision.

Notice the balance achieved through this process. Further, the owner did achieve his goals of reducing his hours and maintaining business as well. Ironically, he was more involved as a leader and less involved in the actual day-to-day tasks of his organization.

Clarify Authority Throughout Your Organization

You can use this basic process to clarify authority in any system. Decision authority must be clarified, work group by work group, throughout your organization. Each decision must be assigned to one person or role, an SPA. *If you do not follow this critical rule, you will create confusion and minimize productivity throughout your organization.* To do this efficiently, use a similar process to the one above, then cascade it, as illustrated below.

Remember, the boss of any group, the person who does your performance evaluation, is also the Sponsor. So decision authority and sponsorship go hand-in-hand.

To illustrate the process, let us revisit the traditional plant structure mentioned earlier.

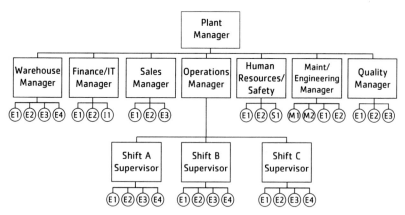

Figure 40 Traditional Plant Example

To start cascading decision authority, you must first admit that it exists; the rest of the steps require work in the form of conversations.

To do this, go work group by work group (boss and direct reports) and cascade the work throughout the organization as illustrated below.

First, *identify the current state.* Be specific about which items, tasks, day-to-day issues, or scenarios require a decision. Delineate who decides and which style is being used for each. Then chart them on the decision grid. Talk about the chart with all employees in the work group to make it as accurate as possible. Then talk about how decision making is working. Does the flow of work happen well, or are there disruptions and times when employees have to wait for decisions to get made in order to do their tasks? Are you achieving your business results?

Second, *develop the future state.* What decisions need to be adjusted in order to create a more efficient workplace? Based on the complexity of change, what time frame makes sense to get there? Make sure to create a plan that ensures each employee is ready and able to take on their new decision authority. They may need training, education, or access to key information in order to make good decisions. (See Appendix E in *CCIO* for the process steps to delegation.)

Some decisions need more managerial involvement. **That's right, decision making is situational;** *many employees need or want more managerial help to make effective decisions.* You can also use the same process with cross-functional items or work groups (see p. 207 of this chapter). Decision-making clarity anywhere increases effectiveness of the whole

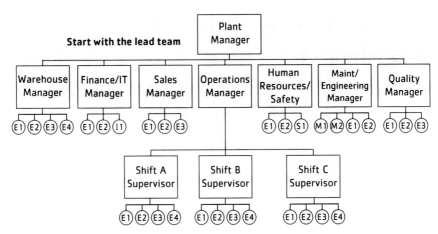

Figure 41 How to Cascade Authority Step 1

organization. Here is how to cascade the process. First, you must start with the lead team as illustrated in Figure 41 on the previous page.

As I noted on page 202, develop the current state, the desired future state, and a plan to get there. Then move to the next group down, as illustrated below, and follow the same process with each work group.

Follow the process all the way to the lowest levels. Almost all employees can identify times when they wait for decisions to be made that they could have made themselves.

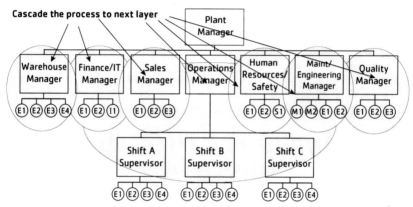

Figure 42   How to Cascade Authority Step 2

To move the whole organization to more clarity and productivity, make sure you do the process with all work groups.

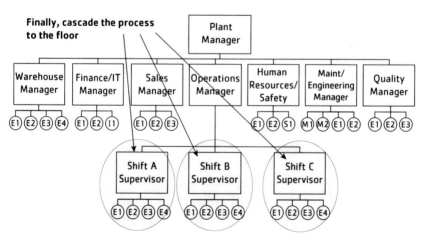

Figure 43   How to Cascade Authority Step 3

Cross-Functional Decision Making

Some decisions run across departments and, therefore, require a different kind of thinking. Many people work in one department: planning, safety, HR, quality, R&D, marketing, maintenance, mechanics, etc., who make decisions that influence others. It is common to have decisions made without input from critical people across functions, who can help ensure the best outcome for the whole organization. Another example of this issue is lack of clarity about who should decide at critical junctures, such as whether to scrap product or to stop a poorly performing machine on the floor. The absence of cross-functional decision-making clarity creates unnecessary workplace conflict.

Most, if not all, workplaces have existing cross-functional areas where daily decisions impact more than one department. Who decides when items run across departments? This is a question that can and should be continually revisited. Often decision processes are put in place to solve moments of crisis, then are never re-examined. Use a similar process as described in this chapter to tweak and continually improve your cross-functional decisions. The grid below was created to do just that.

In reality, all organizations decide "Who decides?" differently. Who makes the call if product gets scrapped, for instance? Sometimes it is the quality auditors and other times the shift leaders? Each workplace

Work Issue Requiring Decision?	Who Decides?	Who is Consulted Prior to Decision?	Who Carries Out the Action?	Who Needs to be Informed?	By When?

Figure 44   Cross-Functional Decision-Making Worksheet

is different; therefore, thoughtful conversations about each unique situation should inform who decides. Use several criteria when choosing who decides: "Who has the best perspective for the entire organization?" (rather than for my department), "Who has the most applicable experience?" "Who has the right technical competency?" etc.

Note: I did not say "highest level leader" as a criterion. It is a misjudgment to think that critical cross-functional decisions should all be made at the highest levels. Instead, use the people who are the most qualified in the particular discipline where the decision must be made.

Notice that the worksheet says "Who Decides?" *Groups don't make decisions, people do.* Key for system health and efficient business operation is gaining decision clarity and continuing to tweak it to achieve and maintain results.

Either use this process in a methodical way, or make sure when you are coaching, directing, and interacting with employees that you are holding the right people accountable. If you are the plant manager, and there are issues in one area that better clarity of decision accountability could help solve, you must hold the right person on your lead team accountable (the Sustaining Sponsor over the area) for driving authority down and changing "Who makes the decision." They must then hold their people accountable, and so on.

If you thwart this principle by directly dealing with the person in that area and lose sight of organization alignment, then you will create confusion and an organization more apt to be misaligned and dysfunctional. Staying in touch with all areas of the organization is critical, but driving clarity of authority and alignment is the path to system health.

Decision Making and Project Governance

Finally, many projects are so large that they need a governing body to help ensure the organization is aligned to the project. Research and Design and IT implementations are typical candidates for this. The basic principles for cross-functional decision making apply here as well as a few other warnings. For one, many create toll-gate systems to manage their R & D projects, or a governing body for IT. Both are good ideas; both have potential traps.

Trap 1—Too cumbersome of a process. Make sure your toll-gate process does not become so large that it handcuffs the system and creates too much extra work just to pass a toll gate. Potential "analysis paralysis" may surface when projects managers spend days or weeks preparing for the toll gate, rather than executing the project. Balance is key. Education is critical, but make sure the governing body has a clear decision process and is not based on consensus. Keep it simple!

Trap 2—Make sure all voices are heard. If the project will have end users such as an IT implementation, *the voice of the end users and location or area managers must be heard as much or even more than the voice of the IT project manager.* In fact, IT should be facilitating the decision process rather than having the loudest voice. Their opinion matters, but only the ends users will know if the system is ready. If they do not know if it is ready, then they have not been educated well enough, so you are at great risk if you decide to start using it. I have seen bad implementations create 50 Percent on-time delivery issues for over a year due to bad governance processes, no alignment, and hard-line attitudes towards end users. The same principles apply to R&D or any other projects that are started in one place but will be implemented at another.

Trap 3—Confusing the governing body with managing people. A solid governing body is critical for educating key leaders and making the best decisions for the project and the organization. Do not confuse that with managing your people. After decisions are made, then leaders need to lead their people and work as hard as ever to communicate and drive the actions forward outside of the governance meetings. Deciding and execution are two different things.

The implementation I mentioned earlier that had 50 percent on-time delivery for a year had only a handful of problems identified at the time of go-live. The Corporate Project Management Office (PMO) was confident at go-live, only to feel distressed when the real problems began to emerge. On the flip side, when I helped implement 40 locations in 4 years, we missed zero shipments while identifying and resolving hundreds of issues at each location. The Corporate Project Management Office was always nervous at the time of go-live due to the amount of issues on our list, but the location leaders were confident that they were prepared for the problems prior to turning on the system, ironically, due to the fact that the project team identified so many issues in communication with the end users.

Software implementation projects proceed in stages, from configuration to testing, and finally "go-live." At each stage, there should be a decision-making process which balances influence from the end users who are helping to configure the system. Including the end users creates a decision matrix between the Business Unit (BU) lead team, the local lead team, the end users, and the project team. Do not allow the project team to make decision recommendations to the BU and location lead team without the voice of the end users.

Decision Governance Process Example

At the end of each implementation stage, end users from each area impacted by the project raised their critical issues to the local lead team. They also indicated whether their area was ready to move forward to the next stage or should take a "time-out" and solve critical issues. The areas included were manufacturing, shipping and transportation, planning, finance and costing, sales, and purchasing. The local lead team weighed the information in terms of overall impact to the location and made their suggestion to the Business Unit lead team, who in turn made their suggestion to the BU president, who then made the final call. The IT project team facilitated the process, along with adding their opinions.

The above process caused several things to happen. First, we did not go live on a few occasions as planned. Second, end users and the location lead team were fully informed of the risk associated with each issue that could have a potentially negative impact on their workplace. When the decision was made to actually go-live, the end users were ready, and in most cases, were actually lobbying to turn the system on.

Clarifying decision making and including the right members in your system is the path to real employee engagement. Please re-read Chapter 9. Once you get that right, then you need to use your personal authority to stay firm and be consistent. If you do this well, you will be rewarded with better results and more committed employees.

Do I Have To, Really?

The conversation continues..

"I've got it, Ed! I know what I have to do!" exclaimed Joe. "I have to be much firmer when it comes to cross-group issues and ensure there is a structure that balances the business. I have been allowing Sally and others to just duke it out; her strength is difficult for the others in the organization to stand up to. Heck, *I* have not even held her accountable, really."

"The first place to start is the ongoing conflict during implementations when a customer says the software doesn't work right. No longer can I allow them to just duke it out. Sometimes it takes months and, really, the decision does not seem to get any better with time. But not making it has killed us."

"Great thinking, Joe!" Tim remarked. "So, who is the best person to make the call? Remember, it shouldn't be the highest level, but the person who, if you had to bet money on it–and you are–would come up with the best solution after talking to people in both departments."

Looking over at Ed, Jane asked, "What is wrong?"

Ed was staring blankly with a white face. "Oh," said Ed, "it's just that I realize how much I contribute to this. I am the 'others' Joe talks about. I often duke it out with Sally. I can see how I have made this worse."

"Tim," Ed said, "you asked the right question, but this is neither the time nor place to answer it. Joe, I have a proposal. I think you, Sally, and I need to have a talk about this. Once, we get on the same page, then an expanded talk can help us come up with the right process. Finding one SPA sounds tricky but, Tim, you did say who must be consulted prior to the decision being made, right?"

"Yes, Ed," replied Tim. "And the 'prior to' should not be taken lightly. In fact, it should be highlighted when setting up the structure. You want your most knowledgeable people, at the lowest levels possible in a dialogue, so that the best decisions can get made for your organization, and also for the customer."

"Ed," Joe added, "nice job! I really admire your self-reflection here. You have definitely been part of the problem. Yet, I let no one off the hook, not even myself. After all, I have been allowing you and Sally to duke it out for a long time. But not any more. I am ready to lead and am clear about the direction. I will take your suggestion to start with some individual conversations, then bring the right people together."

◊◊◊

Later the same week Joe walked into Sally's office . . .

"Hi, Sally!"

"Hi, Joe! What's up?" Sally replied.

"I need to talk to you about a change, and I must say I am a bit worried that you won't like it," Joe said.

"Change," said Sally with some unease.

"Yes," said Joe.

"What the heck are you talking about?" Sally replied. "Are you gonna try and put something over on me?"

"No, Sally. That is not it," Joe replied.

"Well, what the heck is it then?" she inquired.

"It's about how we manage issues between the product manager group and the software engineers," replied Joe.

"Really?" said Sally. "Those idiots are always trying to blame our group for something. If they just learned how to code, then life would be much easier."

"Well, Sally, that is exactly what I am talking about," said Joe.

"Coding?" she said.

"Not coding! The tension you just highlighted by your statement," Joe continued. "It is killing us and it must stop."

"Tension what, are you kidding me?" retorted Sally. "I have worked at a few different places and that tension is always there! Face it, Joe. We are talking about the realities of software development."

"No, Sally," Joe spoke with emotion. "To me, it is the realities of how messed up we are about authority in our organization and how we have learned to over-function to compensate. And you over-function a lot. Yet, you are so good at it that most are afraid of you. Correction: I am afraid of you."

"You?" asked Sally, surprised. "But, you're my boss!"

"Yes, but I am still human, and I was afraid to have this conversation, and afraid to start managing you differently," said Joe.

"Differently?" Sally replied.

"Yes," Joe confirmed. "I have been too permissive with you, Sally. I cannot allow you to do whatever you want. I must ensure that I hold you accountable to a healthier structure and to reaching the goals that I set."

"Hey Joe," Sally retorted. "I am not a kid. Why don't you just treat me like an adult and get out of my way?"

"That is just it, Sally," responded Joe. "I have recently got it that adults are clear about the need for structure and boundaries. A teenage mentality pushes back on being managed."

Sally's anger reached a crescendo, "Teenage?? What are you saying: that it's all my fault? The heck with you!!!"

"Hmmm," said Joe. "I can see why you said that. Actually, I blame myself. I mean the reason you or anyone over-functions is because the system needs it in order to at least get movement. I take accountability for the system that has been created here. After all, I have been in this role for quite some time. Clearly I have been too passive and lacked a systemic focus."

"A what?" said a more calm Sally, "Did you say systemic?"

"Yes." Joe continued, "I am now focusing on each person at each level doing their role, rather than individuals being good and bad. To be clear, I do not want to look over your shoulder and dot the i's and cross the t's, but I do need to hold you more accountable to goals, and that you are managing your people appropriately.

Plus, I cannot have you swooping down and making decisions. I need you holding your managers accountable to make decisions and sometimes coaching them when appropriate. That is not that same as heroic acts to stop lasting conflicts. We need boundaries to ensure our biggest cross-group conflicts have clear strategies to be solved. Then you, I, Ed, or whoever is appropriate, i.e. the Sustaining Sponsor, must be held accountable to make those decisions."

"What?" said Sally. "Do I have to? I mean that sounds like something that I have never experienced and, most of all, it sounds difficult. Plus I have never done it like that before."

"Yes," replied Joe. "But I will be with you each step of the way. Let me fill you in on some things I have been learning." From there, Joe went into depth about his insights from the conversations with Tim.

As Joe was talking, Sally started reflecting on some recent changes she had seen in him. Although she did not quite know why, with this added information *she* was started to think differently about it all.

◊◊◊

A few hours later . . .

"OK," Sally said. "Now what?"

"Now we get with Ed, and—" Joe began.

"Ed? Oh no! Sorry, Joe, but has he put you up to this?"

"No, Sally. This is about my clarity and where I am headed. I need you to come along!"

"Joe, Ed and I always clash. I cannot ever see liking him," Sally remarked.

"Sally, this is about working better together, and if two of my department heads cannot, then how can I possibly imagine the people underneath you will? Besides, I see most, if not all, the fighting is about lack of clarity on who decides. These are systemic issues. I know it is easy to see them as interpersonal, yet they are not. Don't worry, I am holding Ed's feet to the fire just as I am yours."

"Hmmm, OK. But I will hold you to your statement," Sally said.

"Statement? What was that?" said a surprised Joe.

"I don't have to like him." And with that, Sally started laughing. "Actually, Joe, I have nothing against Ed. It is only that our departments clash and we both dig in. Sometimes we fight for months with no resolution."

"Sally," said Joe. "Thanks for your honesty. Yet, each time you fight for even a few days without resolution, it hurts our productivity."

"Wow, Joe," said Sally. "I am embarrassed to admit I understand what you are saying. Yet, often, I really cannot make the call without rounding up the people below me to get the specifics and answers."

"Bingo!" said Joe, "That is why we must create clarity and push the right decisions lower from the beginning."

"OK," said Sally. "So, what is next?"

Joe replied, "Now we must get with Ed and key players from both your departments to identify decisions from the past that got stuck and caused delays or conflicts. For each one we need a clear SPA as well as the right people who should be consulted prior to the decision being made. Your job must shift a bit regarding this dimension; the same with Ed, and others on my staff. You now must ensure that the decision-making structure we create is functioning well and is followed by the employees who report up to you. Additionally, you must help improve any decision areas that are not working by tweaking them until they are running smoothly. Sally, I never want our internal dysfunction to wind up at the customer's door again. Once we take care of our own authority struggles, we will definitely gain an edge on the rest of the competition, and in our market. If clients view us as having superior software as well as being mature and efficient in how we work with them to implement, then we will rock the industry."

"Very good, Joe," said Sally. "I must admit this feels quite uncomfortable to me and, yet, I can see where you are headed."

◊◊◊

A few weeks later Joe stopped by Tim's office . . .

" . . . Then we developed clarity about 15 critical items that we had using the decision-making worksheet (see p. 207). We've already had a few tests of the system. I must say, we resolved a glitch in a few days that sometimes takes weeks, and with minimal tension. To me the product managers and software engineers seem pretty happy. Well, I can see why: we actually gave many of them decision authority on key issues that they could only argue about before. And, Tim, we should have! They are the right people!"

"Wow," said Tim. "I am very impressed. Joe, it take real courage to do what you have done. Nice job."

Joe continued, "Thanks, but I gotta say, many really pushed back hard. I have one person walking around still upset despite the obvious business results which are occurring. Tim, I sort of understand, after all we let people do whatever they wanted for a long time. Yet, it still puzzles me."

"Hmmm," said Tim. "Joe, I could never give you an exact reason. Some people stay disgruntled because life is more complicated than any one theory. Yet, here is a strategy that I've personally found useful to use with people that walk around with chips on their shoulders."

And with that Tim started talking about adult development . . .

◊◊◊

Read Chapter Fourteen

CHAPTER 14

Adult Development

"Once you achieve a certain level in an organization,
you should not have to be managed. Adults should just get along!"
— countless managers and HR professionals

It is no coincidence that people fail to see the relevance of being clear about authority in organizations. We were all born into an authority system called the family. Our primary caregiver(s)' parenting had a profound impact on how we perceive bosses: both in how we manage and how we think we should be managed. Reactive beliefs may persist: rigidity of who can talk to whom, a consensus model pretending all are equal or, worse, the idea that all bosses should be removed.

To think "Adults should just get along" is, ironically, not a very adult statement and is certainly not a higher developmental stage of being. In fact, it speaks more to teenagers, upset at having to care for younger siblings. Of course, mature adults should get along better than most, the majority of the time. In reality, priorities often clash; bosses need clear direction; people have to decide; leaders must lead. *Recognizing the need for bosses to help facilitate all of this is a mature developmental stage for adults.*

Despite this, many organizations have tried to eliminate bosses. In reality, there are no scenarios where a boss does not exist. Somebody is always responsible for performance and will ultimately be held accountable if the organization fails. One sure way to slow an organization, and to render it dysfunctional: have leaderless groups and remove the bosses in the belief that it is a higher level of being. Creating work teams with clarity about authority and roles, with as much autonomy as possible, can yield great results, but it has to be done in a methodical way. Eliminating bosses and pretending that people do not need to be managed is a recipe for an organization to quickly become misaligned.

Instead, create culture change by clarifying expectations of employees on how to work through conflicts better, while handing them more responsibility within parameters. Then provide them with the training and structure to do so. Developmental maturity can happen in humans in terms of interaction skills as well as in technical job capabilities. Ironically, most do not realize this or think that interactive skill development is a waste of time. It is not, but it must be done in a structured evolutionary way rather than by a swift ideological decision. This book is all about how to align your organization to such a change. *Cultural Change in Organizations* is a story complete with a nine-point change strategy to do that very thing.

The Capability to Use Your Authority

Once you are clear about authority and have balanced your structure to help ensure informational flow through the organization (or within your work group and with those groups you either support or get supported by), then you must have the capability to use your authority to hold people accountable. For many this is a struggle. The capability to use your authority, part of the component of personal authority (see Chapter 4: Power) is directly related to your formative years while growing up. "I don't want to be too harsh" or "They better do what I say" are two examples of judgments that cloud people's ability to act as managers. They speak about the speaker rather than the situation. All judgments are remnants of the past spilling into the here-and-now.

Many grew up in households where parents were either too strict and abusive or too permissive and distant. A common reaction is to manage in such a way that is opposite to the style that you liked least as a child, while others hold so tightly to how they were managed as kids that they are inflexible in moments when flexibility is needed or called for.

Balance is the key. The goal is to forgive the injustices of an overdone style (many call these overdone strengths) in your past and learn how to incorporate the positives into your life. Let go of having to "be" a certain way. The ability to be firm and hold people accountable is a critical leader skill, as is the ability to back off and give people space when needed. Effective leaders must also have the capability to appropriately say what they think, and ask for what they want, from all directions, up, down, and sideways.

Of course, if you have the privilege of being a boss, then you also may notice that expectations and judgments get put on you by all your employees that are not really about you. *All employees have authority issues of some kind because all grew up in an authority system called the family (in whatever form it existed).* So, you must be aware of this reality. You will have an unintended impact on your employees at times, for some employees more than others. However, don't allow this dynamic to stop you from using your authority to get work done.

Destructive Entitlement

Some organizations have had years of dysfunction, and have created a workplace filled with passive, mildly upset employees. Those employees are rarely asked about their opinions when solving workplace problems and are often, unjustly, blamed for them. They walk around with a chip on their shoulder and have, rightly or wrongly, distrusted that anything could ever change. They think their behavior is justified by the years of neglect they have received. Family systems therapist Ivan Boszormenyi-Nagy called this chip "Destructive Entitlement."

Change here is possible, but it takes extra patience and persistence. Know that if it took years to create, it will take ample time to fix. All the strategies to clarify authority and get the business aligned in this book are even more important in situations like the one described. But also, as Nagy says "*the cure for destructive entitlement is an appropriate **moment of acknowledgment**"* of the neglect, lack of support, and past injustices that the employees have had to live with. Then, once that acknowledgment has fully happened, it is important to clarify to the employees the new way you are expecting them to behave. In other words, the employee must first be acknowledged for the situation they were in that was tough and that they did not deserve to go through. Then it must also be made clear that the past situation can no longer be used to justify dysfunctional behavior in the present. Be as clear as possible when acknowledging the past, and know that for it to be effective you must be sincere and straightforward;

then clarify the behavioral expectations going forward. Finally, you must hold these people accountable to the new standard and not allow them to be passive anymore.

The mistake often made here, when moving a culture that has been neglected, is to overcompensate and allow dysfunctional behavior to persist. To lead them out of dysfunction, you must begin to be functional and hold your employees accountable to the boundaries and expectations needed to succeed. ***Ironically, appropriate backbone is the solution to a neglected culture.*** That backbone needs to be used to ensure that workers' knowledge is used appropriately to solve problems, and that structures are created so that all voices consistently get heard. Those structures, consistently applied and tweaked, will gradually increase the health of your workplace (see Under-Functioning p. 170).

Once you have been functional over time, the culture will shift, and the workers will move out of their dysfunction. In my experience, however, emotions are often the last factor to come around. Behavioral shifts can happen fast, but emotions seem to lag as employees wait to see if the new current state is a facade or is real. So don't be discouraged if employees are acting differently but verbalizing that nothing has changed.

This Is What Success Feels Like

Several months later . . .

Joe took a deep breath and started to reflect on the year. *Wow,* he said to himself, *I cannot believe what has just happened. In a few short months I have really started being different in my approach and the dividends are starting to pay off. Instead of waiting and only talking to a few people, I have forced difficult conversations and asserted myself in ways that surprise even me. Funny, there are fewer issues-in-crisis coming my way and more problems resolved with well thought-out solutions that are running smoothly. I have had more people frustrated at me than in the past at some of the conversations I initiate, yet the number of people walking in my office upset at the business has dramatically reduced. Most importantly, the business seems to be functioning at a higher level. Wow, by focusing on authority, and aligning people to the difficult mission, we really have made some amazing strides. But perhaps my biggest learning is that if I put in place structures, particularly around project management and decision making on cross-group issues, then those groups function much more efficiently. When that happens, we gain time, energy, and our product is better as a result.* **Therefore, I have learned to use my backbone and authority in ways that I never really realized in order for our business to be functional.** *We are now on target to implement successfully a project that seemed impossible a year ago. Things aren't perfect, but what a change and journey it has been.*

Ed stared up from his desk and noticed Jane walk by. He couldn't help feeling proud of her and all of her recent accomplishments. But he also started thinking about his own journey since she had been hired. *Amazing,* he thought to himself. *I thought Jane was the answer to all our problems when we hired her, yet I have learned that I was looking in the wrong place. I was coached by that funny consultant with the whiteboard and I am now so much clearer about my role in helping align the organization and the software engineers under me on our projects under way. I used to just blame others for the dysfunction I was seeing; now I get it that I play a critical role in working through each issue. Heck, just last week I found out that my blame was way off by having a conversation with the person I was struggling with, much faster than I would have prior to my new learnings. I have also gained a lot of confidence in my work with Joe. It seems like we all are stepping up now and are on the brink of successfully implementing the SMART project after two long years. I thought we could succeed but what I am surprised and excited about is how a systemic focus helps the business. Most important, I have learned a way to use myself to build momentum towards our goals.*

Jane thought she saw Ed staring blankly as she walked by his door. She began to reflect on the year she had since she was hired. First, the struggles with her new assignment, then the added responsibility, and oh yeah, meeting that Tim guy. She smiled. *Wow, what I have learned this year in terms of organizations and projects will last my whole career. I now see my role in creating calm, consistency, and clarity even if others around me seem to be struggling. I always blamed others for my woes, but now I get it that from my position I have a unique view and most importantly, there are specific things I can do to help the difficult conversations happen that ensure success.*

Sally began to reflect. *The last few months have really been a challenge, yet somehow they seemed like progress. I have to admit it, prior to Joe directing me stronger than he ever has, I thought life was great, yet we suffered a lot. Now instead of running around and making the call, I focus on holding accountable the right people who report to me to make the call. Sure I sometimes still have to make the call but, remarkably, decisions are getting made on time. I sort of miss being the maverick, yet I cannot deny that our projects have been moving faster and people seem happier. I was afraid that things would not get done. Yet, I am shocked that, paradoxically, much more has been accomplished. Sure, I may have made some different decisions. Yet, somehow it seems things are working much better.*

APPENDIX A

SATA Assessments

Four assessments follow that are specific to each of the four SATA roles. In step 5 of the SATA analysis on page 100, you were to assess yourself and key Sustaining Sponsor(s) over any areas where you have concerns.

Alignment to work, projects, initiatives, or change is a never-ending task. Work will suffer if you stop paying attention to it. Therefore, use the assessments from time to time to reflect on your and others' key roles. Being well set up in the beginning does not guarantee success.

Instructions—On a piece of paper, rate each of the questions about the SATA roles you have chosen on a scale of 1 to 10, with 10 being high. Use those scores, combined with your knowledge of that person, and your understanding of the project, initiative, or change to develop a strategy to build sponsorship, and align the organization to the work.

Note to Initiating Sponsors—Your job is to make sure that the work of sponsorship for any major initiative is driven through each layer of the organization. The sponsor assessment below focuses mainly on your intact work group. Expand your thinking to make sure you align the whole workplace through your unique leverage as an initiating Sponsor.

Sponsor Assessment

An Excellent Sponsor

1. Clearly communicates both measurable and indirect goals, how they fit into the strategic direction of the business, and which areas will be impacted. Clarity here is tested by whether employees can accurately state the sponsor's goals.

2. Asks for concerns about what may inhibit success, then paraphrase until the employee acknowledges that they are understood. Uses that data to put in place solutions when appropriate.

3. Makes the change a priority with their direct reports and, whenever possible, measures their performance by its success.

4. Organizes their direct reports, key change agents, and targets through appropriate structures to raise and resolve issues, and addresses gaps as needed.

5. Provides the necessary resources (people, time, training, and equipment) to do the work, then monitors and adjusts as needed.

6. Identifies conflict between individuals or other departments and intervenes to resolve them quickly.

7. Insists on periodic follow-up meetings where all accountable for tasks discuss what is and is not working.

8. Is able and willing to deliver both positive and negative consequences.

9. Speaks out appropriately and firmly to employees who question the legitimacy of the work or change.

10. Drives the work until outcome goals are achieved through frequent and consistent monitoring, intervening as needed.

Change Agent Assessment

An Excellent Agent:

1. Seeks to gain clarity about goals of change.
2. Provides ongoing education to the boss about what is happening with the change.
3. Points out behaviors by boss or organization that may hurt the ability to reach the goals of the change by suggesting possible consequences of those behaviors.
4. Is aware of the issues involved and strives to learn about the current state right here, right now.
5. Is clear about the support s/he needs from the sponsor and willing to ask for what s/he wants/needs to be successful.
6. Seeks clarity about the importance of the change with the sponsor and strives to work within those expectations, requirements, and emotional boundaries.
7. Identifies situations that risk the success of the change, such as cancelling a critical follow-up meeting necessary for successful implementation.
8. Encourages Targets to share their ideas, issues or concerns.
9. Views resistance as systemic and invites the sustaining sponsor as well as the targets to work systems issues.
10. Is clear that s/he is not the boss.

Advocate Assessment

An Excellent Advocate:

1. Seeks clarity about who the decision maker for ideas is, i.e., searches for appropriate sponsor.
2. Dialogues with sponsor about current business challenges and generates ideas based on these challenges.
3. Recognizes distinction between giving idea and making decision to implement idea.
4. Clearly articulates ideas as well as perceived benefits and costs.
5. Identifies and communicates ideas, issues, and concerns in a non-blaming way.
6. Recognizes when starting to sell idea versus educating others.
7. If decision to go another direction is made, quickly shifts to contributing ideas that would help create success in that direction.
8. Asks for what she wants in order to be successful.

Target Assessment

An Excellent Target:

1. Seeks to gain clarity about goals of change.
2. Raises priority conflict when boss or change agents are asking him to do things outside of understood priorities.
3. Seeks clarity about distinction between decision-making influence and authority by asking the question: "Who decides?"
4. Seeks decision-making authority, when appropriate, for quick movement without waiting.
5. Asks for what she wants in order to be successful.
6. Identifies and communicates issues and concerns in a non-blaming way.
7. Offers to manage tasks appropriate for his current role.
8. Aids in learning by letting others know when he has changed or corrected another person's work, rather than covering up the problem by doing the other's task without telling them. Thus, the original person can self-correct.
9. Talks directly to, rather than about, others when tension arrives.
10. Contributes ideas.

APPENDIX B

Project Manager SATA Assessment

The following was written working with a research and design group to clarify the qualities and behaviors essential for successful functioning as Project Manager.

Their goal was to work in accordance with SATA in order to align the organization to their projects and ensure success. Written for large cross-functional, mission-critical projects, these principles can and should be adjusted to any size organization.

Instructions—On a piece of paper, assess yourself on each of the following questions, using a scale of 1 to 10, with 10 being high. Then build an action plan to strengthen areas where you scored low.

1. The project manager is sponsored to allocate enough time to interact with all people involved in the project.
2. She has sufficient knowledge of the technical aspects of the project to communicate intelligently.
3. He has sufficient knowledge of the socio-aspects of the workplace to drive clarity of decisions, single point of accountability, roles, lines of authority, and completion dates.
4. She has the personal authority to state opinions in the face of contrary views, while valuing diverse opinions.
5. She has the interpersonal skills to connect with people and to achieve effective communication even in conflict situations.
6. She encourages the continual involvement of the work force and supports an action research approach towards the constant improvement of project plans and steps.

7. He must monitor and WORK the timeline and decision matrix. This means problem solving with people who have actions, checking for clarity, updating the timeline, adding actions (if the timeline is in a computer, the project manager needs to update all involved when any change happens), informing people, educating sponsors, and confronting issues immediately. *This is not a passive role.*

8. She is active, constantly identifying and communicating whether the project is on track, meeting milestones, or slipping due dates.

9. If project is slipping he refocuses the task members or sponsors to get things back on track.

10. She attends to the on-going, continual education of the sponsors about the needs of the project.

11. He is clear that he is NOT the boss. If he finds himself in position of persuading, coaxing, or convincing, he alerts proper sponsors to clarify issues and regain direction.

APPENDIX C

Structure Assessment

Answer each question below using the following scale.

A (almost always), **F** (frequently), **O** (occasionally), **S** (seldom), **N** (almost never)

A. _____ Decision-Making Clarity. I have appropriate authority to do my task. Therefore, I never wait for others to tell me what to do.

B. _____ Single Point of Accountability. There is one person accountable for each task, action, or role.

C. _____ Single Point of Accountability. The person assigned SPA is in the right work group or area for this task, action, or role.

D. _____ By-Whens. Clear dates and times to do tasks and actions are negotiated and agreed upon. When tasks are slipping, those impacted who are dependent on the task's completion get constant feedback.

E. _____ Meetings. My work group meets enough to manage the current situation we are facing.

F. _____ Meetings. The people who have interconnected tasks meet on a consistent basis and the meetings are effective.

G. _____ Measurable Goals. I know what business metrics are impacted by my task and how I am doing against those measures.

H. _____ Priorities. I know what I have to do and its order of importance.

I. _____ Expectations of Work. I am clear about my task and rarely get asked to do things by others who are outside of my responsibilities.

J. _____ Conflict Resolution. When tense moments arise, I know what to do to resolve it and how to create a plan so that the same issue does not repeat itself.

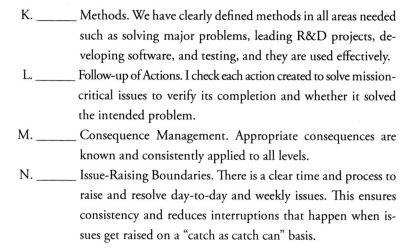

K. _____ Methods. We have clearly defined methods in all areas needed such as solving major problems, leading R&D projects, developing software, and testing, and they are used effectively.

L. _____ Follow-up of Actions. I check each action created to solve mission-critical issues to verify its completion and whether it solved the intended problem.

M. _____ Consequence Management. Appropriate consequences are known and consistently applied to all levels.

N. _____ Issue-Raising Boundaries. There is a clear time and process to raise and resolve day-to-day and weekly issues. This ensures consistency and reduces interruptions that happen when issues get raised on a "catch as catch can" basis.

Rate all categories and build an action plan to improve anything that is "O" or lower. Your workplace is probably suffering if you are not doing the items mentioned on this list at least frequently. The goods news is you have the power to fix it and to significantly improve your workplace.

Please note—If you are a large workplace with major cross-functional projects and initiatives, please re-read Decision Making and Project Governance on page 208.

THE ASSESSMENTS IN
APPENDIX A, ADDITIONAL
SATA EXAMPLES, AND MY
ORGANIZATION DEVELOPMENT (OD)
ROOTS ARE AVAILABLE ONLINE
AT BUSINESS EXPERT PRESS.

Bibliography

Boszormenyi-Nagy, I., and Spark, G. (1973). *Invisible Loyalties: Reciprocity in Intergenerational Family Therapy.* New York: Harper & Row.

Bowen, M., and Kerr, M.E. (1988). *Family Evaluation.* New York: W.W. Norton & Company.

Conner, D. (1993). *Managing at the Speed of Change.* New York: Villard Books.

Crosby, G.L. (2015). *Fight, Flight, Freeze.* Wilmington. DE: CrosbyOD Publishing.

Crosby, R.P. (1992). *Walking the Empowerment Tightrope.* King of Prussia, PA: Organization Design and Development, Inc.

Crosby, R.P. (2011). *Culture Change in Organizations.* Seattle, WA: CrosbyOD Publishing.

Crosby, R.P. (2015). *The Cross-Functional Workplace.* Seattle, WA: CrosbyOD Publishing.

Dewey, J. (1938). *Experience & Education.* New York, NY: Simon & Schuster.

Friedman, E. (1985). *Generation to Generation.* New York, NY: Guilford Press.

Kahane, A. (2010). *Power and Love.* Oakland, CA: Berrett-Koehler

Lewin, K. (1997). *Resolving Social Conflicts & Field Theory in Social Science.* American Psychological Associates

Lippitt, G., and Lippitt, R. (1986). *The Consulting Process in Action.* (2nd ed.). San Diego: University Associates.

Merrill, D.W., and Reid, R.H. (1981). *Personal Style and Effective Performance.* Radner, PA: Chilton.

Minuchin, S. (1974). *Families and Family Therapy.* Cambridge, MA: Harvard University Press.

Rogers, C. (1951). *Client-centered Therapy.* Boston, MA: Houghton Mifflin.

Schmuck, R.A., and Bell, S.E., and Bell, W.E. (2012). *The Handbook of Organization Development in Schools and Colleges.* Santa Cruz, CA: Exchange Point International.

Tannenbuam, R., and Schmidt, W.H. (1958). *How to Choose a Leadership Pattern. Harvard Business Review*, March-April 1958, 36, 2, 95-101.

Whitaker, C.A., and Bumberry, W.M. (1988). *Dancing with the Family.* New York: Brunner/Mazel Publishers.

White, R., Lippitt, R. (1960). *Autocracy and Democracy.* New York, NY: Harpers and Brothers Publishers.

Williamson, D (1991). *The Intimacy Paradox.* New York, NY: Guilford Press.

Chapter Index

*I choose
to show real leadership
in the situations
that I am suddenly
thrust into in life
and
to hold no resentment
for being in them.*

*Instead,
I relish the opportunities,
put forth my best effort,
and thrive!*

CPSIA information can be obtained
at www.ICGtesting.com
Printed in the USA
FSOW02n1656170517
34138FS

9 781631 576607